When a Mustard Seed Grows

From an act of Faith to an act of Congress ©

William J. Marohnic

Iron Sentinel Publishing – Glasgow, KY

ISBN: 978-0-578-64301-4

Library of Congress Control Number: 2020902660

When a Mustard Seed Grows / From an act of Faith to an act of Congress
Digital distribution / Paperback
Iron Sentinel Publishing 2020

Dedication

For all truth tellers who heed the Still Small Voice of their conscience, and dress for battle by putting on the armor of light.

Table of Contents

Introduction

Forty years ago, a remarkable chain of events triggered by a sole act of conscience, occurred in a small town in southern Kentucky. No one would have even taken notice except for the fact that these very local events would soon reach onto a national stage.

In the 1980's the term "whistleblower" was little known. But in rural Kentucky, it became virtually a household word. The circumstances centered on a very public voicing by three mental health professionals working for a community mental health center.

Serious concerns were raised by the three of possible Medicaid fraud and misapplication of mental health services. The alleged misconduct focused on geriatric nursing home programs conducted by the mental health center.

The main issues were false and altered Medicaid billings by the agency claiming treatment services were conducted by professional staff. However in truth, the actual billed services were executed on site in the nursing homes by well-intended paraprofessionals, who for the most part lacked any specialized training and performed with little supervision.

In short, these three newly branded whistleblowers, as coined by the largest state-wide newspaper, were uncovering agency fraud and abuse of the needed mental health treatment services for the infirmed nursing home elderly. No one could have predicted the level of notoriety this human-interest story would garner in the coming months.

Essentially, these very public voicings made by only three, out of an agency staff roster of four hundred; would soon both resonate with and influence action to be taken by lawmakers at the highest levels of government. Ultimately, these actions would reverberate throughout the halls of Congress as well as the highest courts of the land.

The end result would realize a rising tide of legislative and judicial reforms, strengthening First Amendment Free Speech Protections within workplace settings.

Two major government enactments stemming out of actions of the Kentucky whistleblowers were;

1. In 1980 the U.S. Congress passed the Mental Health Systems Act and signed into law by President Jimmy Carter.

    A key provision of the new law was a Whistleblower Protection Amendment sponsored by United States Congressional Representative Tim Lee Carter of Kentucky.

    His advocacy of this amendment was to ensure future protections for government employees who report employer wrongdoing, covering all Mental Health public funding programs in the U.S. On the floor of the House of Representatives, Rep. Carter cited the Kentucky whistleblowers case as justification for the added amendment protections.

2. In 1986 the U.S. Sixth Circuit Court of Appeals Marohnic v. Walker case, further enhanced workplace First Amendment Freedom of Speech protections for employees reporting public agency fraud and abuse.

    Over the next 25 years, the Marohnic v. Walker case judgment has become landmark case law being cited many times in other pending cases before the Federal appellate courts.

Here the historical record exemplifies that the powers of government can work on behalf of the common citizen to serve the greater good in the public interest.

However, as important as these enactments are, they pale in comparison to the underlying spirit which resonates much deeper than mortal men seeking secular legalisms by adherence to the "narrow letter of the laws."

Rather, the pursuit of the "spirit of the law" by conscience driven mortals emanates from a much higher calling harkening back to the Old Testament where God himself proclaims, "I will write my laws upon your hearts."

Furthermore, a higher calling often demands change i.e. righting a wrong. Oftentimes, the obligatory changes may come with a high personal cost.

Moreover, man by himself without Divine inspiration often fails to reach the higher moral ground of victory. Here in our story, to be a whistleblower one must not have a faint heart. Exposing employer graft and corruption would result in navigating choppy uncharted waters far from safe harbors.

The 18th century poet Winfred Garrison in his book, **Thy Sea So Great: A Book of Verses**, famously captures the whistleblower's dilemmas, "Oh God, thy sea is so great and my boat so small."

Yet surprisingly, at their lowest ebb of uncertainty and anxiety, a faint light began to perforate through their darkness. The renowned minister and philosopher Ralph Waldo Emerson penned in **Self-Reliance**, " men should watch for and detect that sudden flash of light crossing the mind;" for it may be a God whisper, as the inner voice of conscience awakens and stirs the human spirit, which inspires both thoughts and deeds to elevated heights reaching benevolent ends.

At the conclusion, the power of conscience lights their uncertain path, eventually prevailing over the darkness.

Hence, let us begin our story at the beginning.........

Chapter I

Baptism of Fire

Upon earning a Master's Degree in Social Work in 1975, I began a professional career as a Therapist with a Community Mental Health Center in Kentucky. Assigned to the Geriatric Program, I would work with clients in nursing homes. Working with elderly was not my first choice as a vocation. In graduate school, I did my field practicum in prison settings. The criminal justice system was my logical choice. During my field placement I was an intern at a minimum security prison outside Lexington, Kentucky. My project was working with prisoners in compiling a Rights and Responsibilities Policy Manual which would be used by the prison Warden and staff. Representing the prison population in this project, gave me a unique view from the Warden's office. It was my first real lifework experience as a Social Worker.

Shortly after beginning work at the prison, I was interviewing a prisoner who was to assist me in ways to relate to the others incarcerated. I asked him what he had done which resulted in his imprisonment. He responded, "Murder." I was actually having lunch with a man who had taken the life of another human being. I then realized what a greenhorn I was!

As I entered the real workforce, I was young, idealistic, filled with energy and commitment, believing nothing to be beyond my grasp. I was excited to be working within an agency that I believed to be on the cutting edge of providing critical and essential mental health services to large and diverse groups of needy people. Also, I was eager to work with staff of various professional disciplines who shared my idealism, similar to my college colleagues. The sense of purpose and conviction among fellow students, I found to be intoxicating and believed, the same, would naturally carry over into the real world work environment. So at the age of twenty-seven, and married with two small children, I began my journey filled with hope and promise.

The Community Mental Health Center was one of fifteen located throughout Kentucky. These regions were established in the 1960's when the Community Mental Health Center Federal Legislation was passed and signed into law by President John F. Kennedy. This law focused on community based mental health treatment as opposed to the earlier model of large inpatient mental hospital settings. The premise being, dealing with mental health issues at a local level would be more effective. The earlier hospitalization setting did little to help the individual in better coping with daily living problems encountered in the more natural environment of the community.

Therefore, during the 1960's thousands of previously hospitalized mentally ill people were discharged into the community. The community based outpatient treatment centers were needed to provide service for this influx of high risk individuals.

In Kentucky, these fifteen Centers were funded primarily with Federal monies. The Medicaid Program was a major funding source for the Centers, and made up a large portion of their budgets. The Centers divided their clientele into mental health and mental retardation programs. There were outpatient mental health programs, sheltered workshops, drug and alcohol programs, adult day care, and geriatric services for the nursing home elderly. The Centers hoped to develop and grow a self-pay client system, with more funds coming from private resources and private insurance with the long term goal being to wean the Centers off public funding by shifting more to private sources. However, when I began working for the Mental Health Center, there remained a heavy dependence on public funding.

My initial job assignment was providing counseling services to elderly nursing home residents. I was provided a staff of three paraprofessionals to assist me in the delivery of care. My first visit to a nursing home was quite disturbing and uncomfortable. There was a slight odor of urine that filled the rooms and hallways. Many residents were in their rooms, sitting in a chair or lying on the bed. Other residents were sitting quietly in a common lobby area in a small group. I was introduced as, "the new Therapist", to several residents, who appeared to be detached from the immediate situation, returning only a blank stare. The nursing home was very large, with many people coming and going, but there was quietness amidst so much activity. Many resident faces lacked emotion or expression. It was a depressing experience, leaving me with a sense of hopelessness and futility.

I had done some homework, and was aware of several studies indicating as many as seventy to eighty percent of the elderly suffer from some kind of mental illness or impairment. The studies discussed the lack of treatment interventions available to this high risk group.

After a couple of months, I began to feel more comfortable with my job. I worked in a small town with a population of approximately five thousand people. At the center of town was the Courthouse square. The daily pace was slow and laidback. Our office was located in the City Hall building and consisted of three small offices and a reception area. The three paraprofessionals, who were my staff, were young women in their twenties and thirties. They were friendly and hardworking, but untrained as mental health workers.

We had three nursing homes under contract for group services which were conducted twice weekly. Each nursing home had fifteen to twenty residents who had been designated by the Mental Health Center staff, and approved by the nursing home Administrator to participate in the group sessions. Each resident had a Medicaid card, which the Center billed twice weekly for the service provided.

At that time, each billed service paid by Medicaid was $16.82. The nursing home also received $16.82 Medicaid reimbursement for twenty-four hour care. The Center received the same payment rate from Medicaid for the group therapy session which would have the duration of one to two hours. Center employees were instructed not to share this billing information with the nursing home staff. However, some nursing home Administrators' would learn of the reimbursement arrangement with the Mental Health Center and seemed to harbor resentment that the Center received the same compensation as the nursing home for a program lasting only a couple of hours.

My college studies did not include treatment modalities tailored to the Geriatric age group, so at first I felt awkward, and very much the novice, in my clumsy attempts to deliver meaningful service. It was difficult to penetrate the solid wall of detachment I encountered, but slowly cracks developed, leaving openings to small communications, facial gestures and eye contact. During these early encounters, I could sense a cloak of suspicion and distrust directed to me. I persisted with expressions of cordiality, kindness, and treating each as my equal, never talking down to them. I felt this was the key to slowly reaching them. I became more convinced that through one to one rapport, inroads could be made to break through the barriers erected. With time, I gained confidence, becoming more comfortable and effective with my treatment attempts. I began to realize this age group of "captive clients" had unique emotional and mental problems which impacted them in addition to the obvious physical issues. Often these emotional problems were professionally labeled as, "adjustment reactions to the aging process." But what I saw in my clients was more basic, more down to earth. To me, these were individuals who had lived long lives, acquiring a portfolio of vast life experiences worthy of celebration and recognition. They often were sick and confused, but you could still see in their eyes or demeanor that special grace and dignity that results from many years of just living life.

One of my clients was quite special. In her later 80's, she was immaculate in her appearance, confined to a wheelchair, and did not speak. She often dressed in homespun attire, some light jewelry adorning her dress, neatly coifed hair with earrings, and a touch of lilac scented perfume. In spite of the overwhelming effects of aging, her feminism was still evident. She captured the Southern gentility of her earlier upbringing and life. Her image remains with me to this very day and represents the reason the elderly are entitled to proper care and services which enable them to close their lives in comfort and with dignity.

Breaking the ice with the elderly men was also difficult. They too, seemed withdrawn and detached from the environment. I can recall many sit down chats, which would result in the release of pent-up emotions and memories, slowly bringing each back to life. Humor, smiles, and laughter would brighten their faces. This was quite a contrast from what I had observed only weeks earlier.

The change in their social interactions did not stem from any highly skilled treatment techniques. In short, I believe any improvement was a result of human contact based on respect, kindness, and simply spending time with them. The one-to-one sessions I had with the elderly residents convinced me that the treatment focus should shift away from the group arts and crafts type programs, and concentrate more on individual counseling. However, individual counseling needed to be injected into the treatment planning for most of the clients enrolled in the program. Individual counseling had to be done by a licensed nurse, social worker, or clinical psychologist. I began to do as many one-to one sessions as time would permit in an eight hour work day. It became obvious to me, that additional professional staff was needed in the Geriatric Program in order to provide the individual attention needed to realize the same result I was seeing in my client population.

At the end of the first six months on the job, I assessed my situation. I was enjoying my work, making a decent living, acquired a promotion, and began to feel as though I had found my calling. There were also storm clouds on the horizon that eventually would turn my world upside down and force me on a path that would alter my life forever.

I began to notice two disturbing trends becoming increasingly evident; the first being, a "professional snobbery" attitude coming from the top management regarding the Geriatric programs and the assigned staff. Any form of services provided in these programs were dismissed as not clinically relevant and not worthy of being delivered by other more professionally trained and educated staff.

The second trend centered on the money-making features of the Geriatric Programs. Because the services were provided to a captive group audience, they generated substantial funds for the Center. These economic influences were impacting the Agency during a period where financial problems existed and other Agency programs were running in the red.

Consequently, there was a demand from top management to increase the frequencies of nursing home programs, enroll additional clients, and recruit new nursing homes. As these programs expanded, the only additional employees hired were untrained paraprofessional staff, rather than the credentialed therapists I had hoped the Center would recruit.

At the outset, I understood that each billed service was to be delivered and/or supervised by a professional therapist. The paraprofessional was an integral part of the service delivery team and their work would be directly supervised and "signed-off" by the attending professional. The Medicaid regulations were being loosely interpreted by the Agency and this resulted in a grey area as to who should actually provide the service. My supervisor established a policy that the professional would review the notes written by the paraprofessional, and by co-signing their note entry, the service was legitimate. In short, the beginnings of a "Medicaid mill" were taking form, causing me concern.

One day, upon arrival to the office, the scene before me resembled an assembly line at the local factory. Rented typewriters lined a long work table and clerical staff was busy removing staff note entries from client medical records and replacing the handwritten note with a new typed note.

The new typed medical record entry deleted the signature of the paraprofessional and replaced it with space for the signature of a professional therapist only. The handwritten entries were being destroyed. As the service volume increased, stretching the professional to be present at all services in progress was impossible. The assurance voiced by Agency management that this practice met regulatory requirements, failed to alleviate my uneasy feeling. This practice continued for six months, involving three large rural counties and ten to fifteen nursing homes.

In addition, I was feeling more and more troubled with my supervisor. He seemed to be a well-intentioned professional, but appeared insecure in his job. He was prone to panic and often anxiety ridden. He constantly worried about pleasing his supervisors and was overly obsessed with losing his job. These behavioral problems often led to erratic decision making.

My growing concerns soon came to a head on the day he came to the office and informed me that he was increasing the number of nursing home programs provided in my region. I did not have to attend any of these services, but would be required once a week to go to each county office, review the staff notes, and sign-off on the services provided. Although I was not required to be present for the program, I would be expected to sign-off on each service as meeting clinical and professional standards.

I informed him that I could not lend my signature, as a professional, for services which I had no involvement. He defended this directive as being essential financially for the Agency and if not executed, massive personnel lay-offs would result. I told him I needed additional time for consideration and would get back with him the following day.

I had a sleepless night, realizing my dilemma. If I refused, I believed I could be fired, yet if I agreed to this new directive, I would be lending my professional credentials to a possibly fraudulent billing scheme. That could end my career. Also, I knew the elderly would be cheated of essential mental health services needed to address problems of depression, disorientation and even psychosis. I felt they were being used in an elaborate money making scheme.

The next morning I decided to send a memorandum to Dick Hayes, my supervisor, and the Associate Director, his supervisor, stating I could not lend my professional credentials to this program expansion. I would limit my delivery of services to fewer nursing homes where I could insure quality of care and felt more comfortable of being in compliance with the Medicaid program. Three days later, I received a call from John Johnson, the Associate Director, instructing me to report to his office later that day. I was certain I was going to be terminated for refusal to comply with the directive of my immediate supervisor.

Upon arrival to the meeting, I was surprised that my supervisor was present and he was cordial. The Associate Director told me he was unaware of the expansion plans and agreed with me that if implemented, we would be out of compliance with the Medicaid regulations. He also stated he was making some personnel changes which involved my supervisor being promoted to a new position, removing him from the nursing home programs. I was asked to take responsibility as Geriatric Supervisor and pursue new directives to improve the quality of treatment services, which included hiring additional professional staff. I was elated; accepted the new job assignment, and congratulated Dick on his promotion.

With the promotion to Geriatric Supervisor, my role expanded to supervision of a five county area with fifteen nursing homes. The contracts with the nursing homes were already in place with the Agency and were classified by the State as Personal Care Homes and Intermediate Care Facilities. The number of clients per facility averaged about twenty, with a diverse range of mental impairments ranging from simple senility to various degrees of psychosis. As previously, the services provided by the Agency were mostly group sessions, loosely conducted by a therapist with a supporting cast of paraprofessionals or aides. This modality of service delivery, with a mix of therapist and aides, created a grey area in meeting the Medicaid regulatory guidelines. For reimbursement purposes, the group intervention had to be provided by or under the direct supervision of a licensed social worker, a psychiatric nurse, a clinical psychologist, or a psychiatrist. This grey area led to growing numbers of billing rejections, which resulted in the increasing issues of Agency non-compliance with Medicaid regulations.

This was an on-going problem I had to address. I would have to increase the clinician input and decrease the paraprofessional involvement in actual treatment intervention. The paraprofessional had an important role in the nursing home programs. They gathered the participants for the group, provided needed visual aids, planned and assisted with the activity, and passed out food treats. They made some medical record entries, completed the billing documents, and performed various clerical duties. The role of the therapist was to conduct the group session, provide individual client interventions as needed, and do the bulk of the medical record documentation.

I needed to restructure the compliment of the staff in order to eliminate the confusion as to who actually provided the service to the client. Some of the paraprofessionals would need to be let go or reassigned to strictly clerical -activities, in order to free-up funds for hiring credentialed staff. The Geriatric Program was producing a budget surplus, which should be helpful in my attempts to secure additional professional staffing. Additionally, there had to be changes with the group therapy format. More focus was needed on designated treatment objectives and less emphasis on arts and crafts. All the treatment plans needed to be updated and restructured by the therapists. There was a need to return to handwritten medical record entries by the clinician, rather than the typed entry done by the aides. Until the additional professional staff could be recruited and hired, and the other changes put into place, the frequency of programs would need to be reduced.

I approached my direct supervisor, John Johnson, with my analysis of the program and the changes I believed were needed to insure quality treatment and regulatory compliance with Medicaid. John would present my proposals to the Executive Director and let me know if I had the green light to proceed.

A week or so passed, and then John informed me that my proposals were still under advisement. He said the Executive

Director had insured Medicaid officials that new reform measures were taking place in the Geriatric Program further insuring quality of care. Upon hearing this, I was optimistic that I would be hiring additional professional staff soon. During this time, I still maintained a caseload of nursing home clients in addition to my program administrative duties.

Things became more frustrating for me, as daily I witnessed the Outpatient Clinic therapists having a lot of down time due to their very light client schedules. They managed to occupy the day with staff meetings, extended lunch hours, and early work day departures. Meanwhile, my Geriatric staff was working hard. I raised these concerns and suggested that some of these clinicians' could assist in the nursing homes. I was informed that these Outpatient therapists' felt uncomfortable about going to the nursing homes and believed the elderly would not be responsive to their forms of therapy. Also, it may cause administrative problems in charging their time to different programs. This seemed lame to me.

It was apparent that the professional snobbery was much more widespread that I had realized earlier. Providing therapy services to an aged person in a nursing home setting, was disturbing to most of the Clinic therapists who preferred the "Madison Avenue" concept of limiting their contact to upper-class, private pay clients. This was an unrealistic view of how Community Mental Health Centers operated within the state of Kentucky. Most outpatient clients receiving treatment were on public assistance or welfare and often had drug related problems. Over the years, the outreach efforts to target the upper and middle class groups for outpatient psychiatric services had been largely unsuccessful. This fact did not deter the Outpatient therapists' from resisting having any change made with their job role.

They argued that due to the issue of senility, most associated with the elderly, there could be no positive response to psycho-therapy. This was true for the minority of nursing home residents with organic brain syndrome; however, even this group could benefit from a wide range of reality therapies. Most of our geriatric clients had the same form of psychosis, depression, obsessive-compulsive behaviors, etc., as the younger age population within the community. Many were depressed due to advancing health problems and the loss of independence, which tore them from their home, bringing them to the nursing home. A sense of abandonment haunted them because of the death of spouses and infrequent or no visits from family. These circumstances create fertile ground for despair. Unaccustomed to living with a large group of strangers, some were suspicious or paranoid of other patients, who they feared would harm them. Most often these fears were baseless, but nevertheless, very real to the afflicted individual. Sexual acting out, was also behavior which was responsive to therapeutic intervention. Indeed, the nursing home elderly presented a wide and vast spectrum of treatable and reversible conditions that, from my observations, cried out for intervention.

The Agency had the professional resources to address these human needs, but lacked the compassion and commitment to do so. The Outpatient therapists' discriminatory attitudes and apathy toward dealing with the elderly, was in fact what barred their involvement in the Geriatric nursing home program. Upper management never challenged these attitudes, so things went on as usual. Qualified therapists' continued with an assignment to idle Outpatient offices, with the Agency relying on "profit center" programs such as Geriatrics' to carry the financial load.

Finally, I was authorized to initiate an employment search for two professional social workers. Other departments were under a hiring freeze as the Agency was plagued with increasing financial problems. In addition, housekeeping measures to reduce operating costs Agency wide were made mandatory. It was a disturbing time of uncertainty and low staff morale. After months of surveillance, I had observed enough of how the Agency operated to know that some programs and departments were "sacred cows" and others, like the Geriatric Program were treated like step children. The sacred cow programs had bloated budgets, but were not expected to be solvent. The Outpatient Clinic programs were the most sacred cows of them all. These departments were top heavy with highly paid master level clinical psychologists. The clinic offices, conference room facilities, and supportive clerical staff, added to the high program costs. The clinic therapists' believed they were the Agency elite, and entitled to special status in the pecking order. Other departments and programs, such as Geriatrics, Adult Day Care, and the Sheltered Workshops were considered second tier, managed by less prestigious professionals such as social workers' or registered nurses'. These programs were solvent, and these profit centers needed to carry the load of the sacred cow programs. This agency dynamic placed added stress on the programs realizing a profit, to over produce. The program imbalance and disparity was blatantly obvious.

I no doubt, began to feel the same kinds of fiscal demands and pressures as my predecessor. However, I felt a need to strike a balance between these monetary pressures and the delivery of a quality service. I was dedicated to insuring that the Geriatric Programs under my supervision were run in a professional manner. I witnessed earlier, how out of control policies bent solely on income generation, could end in near disaster. The Geriatric Program was self-sufficient and could afford a proper therapist-client ratio in order to treat this high risk group with some degree of success, if given equal status with other Agency programs.

Concerns grew worse when my boss John Johnson, told me he was leaving the Agency, having accepted a position as Executive Director with a Mental Health Center in the state of New York. I would miss him. John supervised with a steady hand and was not prone to erratic decision making. With his departure, I would be placed under the direct supervision of the Executive Director. I remembered Dick telling me that the Executive Director was "calling all the shots" with the problems we had encountered earlier with treatment quality and excessive Medicaid billings. This made me apprehensive about what the future might bring.

Chapter II

Rise and Fall: *Flashpoint*

With some anxiety, 1978 began as a promising year. I initiated the process of hiring two additional mental health professionals to work within the nursing home programs. My objective was to improve the quality of mental health services for the elderly. Direct treatment services provided by credentialed professionals with paraprofessionals assisting would insure a superior service in addition to reestablishing the Agency's credibility with State and Federal Medicaid officials.

During this time, I was asked by the Agency's Executive Director to go to the State Capital and meet with Medicaid representatives for the purpose of outlining the reform changes I was making with the nursing home programs. During a series of meetings, I assured the officials we were upgrading the quality of care by increasing the number of professional staff assigned specifically to the Geriatric Program Unit. I was feeling a growing level of trust developing from State Medicaid representatives and consequently there was a significant decrease in the number of service billing inquiries from the State to the Agency.

I recall an incident involving $30,000 of billed Medicaid services which were being questioned by the State and I was designated by the Executive Director to go to the Capital to reassure the Medicaid regulators' that we were in compliance with the

Medicaid guidelines. Following a two hour meeting, the officials' agreed to release payment for the services to the Agency, making it clear that they held me responsible for future compliance. They had my assurance that services provided and billed would be to the letter of the law. I remember the relief expressed by the Executive Director when I called him following the meeting to inform him that the $30,000 check was in the mail. He said that money insured meeting payroll for the entire Agency.

Also, I had begun attending weekly Management Staff Meetings which were conducted by the Executive Director and included program Department Heads. I was the Department Head for Geriatric Nursing Home Programs across the Agency. My earlier concerns about sacred cow programs resurfaced. During these meetings, I began to feel I was not considered an equal with other Agency program Department Heads.

I believed the main reason for this disparity was because my programs focused on the elderly. As touched upon earlier, this age group did not rise to the level of importance reserved for outpatient psychiatric/mental illness clients, and were viewed as being senile, un-kept, zombie like persons who were unresponsive to treatment. Most outpatient clinicians' viewed it being beneath their talents and training to be involved in a nursing home group program.

At one of these Management Meetings, I was asked in a joking way, if we had enough warm milk and cookies for the next nursing home program. It was this prevailing attitude of other professional management staff that motivated me to present a specialized Geriatric In-Service Training Session to feature improved treatment planning and better record keeping. I had the impression that Geriatric Services were viewed by the Agency as a stepchild program with a value solely for revenue generation to support the sacred cow programs provided by more elite professionals. As Geriatric Director, it became my mission to reverse this bias through recruitment of additional professionals who were dedicated and committed to counseling the elderly in nursing homes.

In April, I was offered a promotion to an Associate Director Position. This was quite a surprise to me. My duties would be expanded to include Outpatient Mental Health, Mental Retardation, and Developmental Disabilities programs for a five county service district. I retained my role as Regional Geriatric Supervisor as the agency's ten county service area. I was now considered by others to be the Director's "fair-haired boy."

No one had risen within the Agency so quickly to an upper management position. They felt that I had no business being promoted to the slot just below the Executive Director, especially since my background with the Agency was limited to supervision of the Geriatric Programs. Now they had to report to me and they did not like it. This promotion required relocation to a regional office in a rural area of South Central Kentucky. The Executive Director informed me that this office was primarily a center for Outpatient Service delivery staffed with a number of Clinical Psychologists. The programs had a low level of productivity and consistently ran in the red.

There was a large Geriatric Service Program that was well-run and not subject to the Medicaid problems I had encountered earlier. The atmosphere of the office was laid-back with business being slow. Rumors were abound about staff having light work schedules, reporting to work late and leaving early. I was told staff would wash their cars in the Agency parking lot during office hours.

My earlier concerns about working directly with the Executive Director eased. We appeared to be on the same page about improving the quality of services provided to the nursing homes. One day I had lunch with the Director. He discussed the earlier problems with the Medicaid regulations and implied that Dick was a "loose cannon" who made several improper decisions which placed the Agency in jeopardy with the State. He said he had removed Dick from any supervisory responsibility with the Geriatric Program, once he became aware of the damage which had occurred.

I voiced my concerns about the low productivity I perceived with the Outpatient Clinics. To my surprise, he agreed that this issue was becoming a growing burden for the Agency. However, the problem was hard to reverse due to the unified opposition from the psychologists to any major changes.

Nevertheless, everything was falling into place for me. The Geriatric Program across the entire Agency was starting to take shape. With the addition of new professional staff and improved in-service training sessions, I felt we were exceeding Medicaid standards. I increased the role of the Geriatric Supervisor for District Two. Madelyn was a Psychiatric Nurse and a confident professional who ran an efficient program. She was instrumental in blending the two separate Districts together with a more uniform and effective delivery of Geriatric services. However, I was still struggling with the problem of low productivity within the Outpatient Clinics. Overall, I was very pleased with my new role as Associate Director. The trappings of the office were enticing. My salary had more than doubled in eighteen months. I was the number two man in the Agency, with considerable authority. My future looked bright.

As Associate Director, I continued to stress a need for increased Outpatient productivity. I established a goal of four client interventions per therapist per day. Previously, each therapist averaged only two sessions daily, making the work load light for clerical staff as well as the clinician. This new policy goal was not well received and met with resistance, overtly and covertly, on a daily basis. For nine months tension persisted between the professional staff and me due to philosophical differences regarding work productivity and ethical treatment of clients.

During that summer of 1979, we lost our building lease and consequently had to move. One of the Agency's Board members owned an office complex on the other side of town, and he was more than willing to enter into a long term rental agreement with the Agency. This was going to be a big ordeal. Office equipment, client medical records, and furniture had to be moved. It took an entire week to make the move.

In my new office several file cabinets were in need of clearing out materials left by my predecessor. Following months of procrastination, I finally set about completing this task. While sorting through the files, I came across a thick folder labeled, "MEDICAID PROGRAM 1977-1978". The folder contained several letters addressed to the Agency Executive Director along with a thick bundle of copies of Medicaid billing forms with a large "REJECTION" stamp imposed on each billing which the Agency had submitted to the State Medicaid program. The substance of the letters focused on the Agency's Geriatric Programs being in non-compliance with Medicaid State and Federal regulations. The correspondence informed the Agency that billed treatment services appeared to have been provided by paraprofessionals rather than required certified professional staff. The billings amounted to approximately 4,000 submissions covering a four month period. The billings were for a three county area of nursing homes from my former district. Upon closer examination, I discovered my professional billing code listed as being the service provider. The State had requested a sampling of staff note entries to be submitted to the Medicaid program for audit. A copy of a letter from the Agency's Executive Director agreeing to the submission of the specified documentation, and expressing his hope of clearing the matter so payment to the Agency would be approved, accompanied the rejected billings. Additional memoranda indicated Medicaid approval of payments for hundreds of prior rejected claims under the criteria that these services were conducted by a certified professional and the billing professional code submitted by the Agency was mine!

I reviewed the dates of services and the listed nursing homes and there was no question that I had reviewed the staff notes entered by the paraprofessional and co-signed the note to confirm the service met treatment plan objectives. The notes did not validate that I had personally delivered the service, yet the Agency submitted them for payment based upon services they knew to be non-compliant. The vision of the typewriter assembly line popped into my mind, it suddenly occurred to me that the purpose for typing the medical record entries to replace the hand written notes was to cover the fact that the service had not been provided by a credentialed professional. Typed medical record notes would imply the service was provided by the person signing the entry, and in the case of these billing submissions, that person signing was me.

With over 4,000 billing submissions, the payout could be over $70,000! In short, my professional credentials and professional license was in jeopardy if audited, and the Agency, no doubt, would make me the fall guy. I left work filled with anguish, anger, and outrage. I considered confronting the Executive Director with the file of documents I had stumbled across, but believed he would simply shrug it off, tell me not to worry about it, and proceed to make plans to force me out of the Agency. I knew the information contained in that large file would be damaging to the Executive Director and potentially costly to the Agency.

Pondering my options, I considered forgetting about it and stashing the file in the back of an obscure cabinet. I was doing quite well in the Agency, getting the promotion to Associate Director in just eighteen months, and being thirty years old my future seemed very promising. Just a few years ago, I was a high school dropout working at a large chain grocery store in South Florida. I was on a career track of becoming a store manager, but realized that my future would be limited. I needed to make my life count; I wanted to make some kind of contribution to society. I sought guidance and direction for my life from God. It became apparent to me that some kind of Devine Providence took control of my life at that point. A sense of purpose focused my efforts toward education. I studied for, and received my high school diploma, enrolled in Junior College completing a B. A. Degree, and was accepted into the Social Work program at the University of Kentucky, obtaining a Master's Degree in Social Work. These years involved much financial struggle, family sacrifice, and stress.

Suddenly, I'm in the present, facing a decision that I knew had to be made which would have ramifications on my life. I knew that this was a clear cut case of Medicaid fraud that took place over at least a year, involving thousands of dollars, dozens of unknowing and innocent people. I was caught right in the middle of this Medicaid mill! I should have been more perceptive as to what was happening at an earlier stage. I realized my own earlier shortcomings relating to Medicaid compliance, or the lack of compliance, was resurfacing to bite me.

From the day I was hired, a constant state of confusion as to what the Medicaid regulations constituted billable caregivers, kept the Geriatric Program in a state of flux. Looking back over time, it now seemed to have been a deliberate attempt to maintain this "grey area" which resulted in the increased use of paraprofessionals in delivering and billing the State for services. It was easy to limit inquiry relating to the administrative details, and simply accept the policies and procedures handed down. The heavy focus on arts and crafts sessions with little attention given to therapeutic treatment interventions had become disturbing for me. I also felt I was unable to supervise the services effectively because I was stretched too thin.

Eventually, I caught on to what was happening and refused to participate any further. My biggest regret was I should have pushed back much earlier. Now it was apparent to me, that the Agency quietly tried to re-submit Medicaid billings and altered medical records for a three to six month period. The evidence of this attempt was the thick files of Medicaid billing rejections and the audit inquiries from the State, which lay before me on my desk.

When it became obvious I had acted, and changes were put into place. However, now I understood the reality of what had taken place, and also realized this circumstance would force me to make a decision which would possibly change my life and the lives of others forever. This struggle of conscience really began to wear on me. I resented this happening to me. Why couldn't my life be more like other staff who seem to coast along enjoying the daily benefits of their jobs and feathering their nest with very little downside. Yet, I knew that this was wrong. It was stealing from those clients that were the most vulnerable; stealing tax payer money funding services that were not rendered and unwittingly placing innocent people into deceptive schemes to commit fraud. This was only one small agency located in a rural part of the country defrauding the government of thousands of dollars. Nationwide, this practice could involve millions of dollars and deprive thousands of high risk elderly of essential mental health services.

I thought of the old saying, "the truth shall set you free." However, I also remembered hearing, "but it will be very painful." This summed up my dilemma perfectly. I always considered myself to be a good Christian, wanting my life to be a positive contribution, but I never gave much thought of having to pay a price for it. In graduate school, the operative term was to be "a change agent". No mention was given about personal cost or sacrifice required, in exchange for the desired outcome. This is where the pain comes in. I was unsure if I had the will or courage to face the pain. The one thing I knew was there would be a lot of pain, and perhaps for a very long time.

In my mind, I continued to debate the pros and cons of speaking out. After all, this was a small agency in the hinterland of rural Kentucky. The amount of fraud was not that much, and making a big deal about this may not change anything. Most stories I had heard about whistleblowers did not end well. Often times, the wrongdoing continued with only personal and career damage for those who spoke out. I also knew, this was not an innocent, incompetent blunder by the Agency. The resubmission of these billings was a deliberate act. They could not plead ignorance regarding the Medicaid regulations. They were instructed by the Medicaid officials as to the specific guidelines, and several times reminded in writing, of compliance standards.

The Agency continued to ignore the guidelines, and used unqualified personnel to deliver services and bill the State improperly. Even worse, billing forms and medical records had been altered, in order to receive public funds by fraud and deception. This endangered the professional licensure of the therapist by using their credentials in an unlawful manner.

I could not accept these agency indiscretions lightly. The total disregard or honesty and lawful behavior were incredulous, not to mention the breech of ethics and integrity. I also felt I was a poor choice to be the one to speak out. I was not an experienced administrator; not much more than a rookie. I was just starting my career, and since the promotion to Associate Director, not very popular with the staff. I knew I was no match in taking on the Executive Director and the entire Board of Directors.

The Board membership was voluntary in nature. The members received no compensation. To their credit, they took the time to get involved in mental health issues within their communities. The composition included teachers, lawyers, farmers, business owners and housewives. I knew, my reporting of fraud to the State, would put them on the defensive and they would likely give full support to the Executive Director. This public disclosure of wrongdoing would be a major embarrassment for the Board, the Agency, and the community.

I found myself at a crossroad. I always considered myself to be a team player, not a crusader and certainly never a whistleblower. I preferred to avoid conflict and not rock the boat. I knew the Agency had a checkered history with upper management staff who dared to disagree with the Executive Director. He was an aggressive individual and could be very intimidating. At times, he was pleasant; perhaps even charming, but one was ill advised to cross him. He also had political connections at the State Capital and was never reluctant to use these connections to serve his interests.

The result of confronting or challenging the Director's authority almost always led to career implosion and ruin for the challenger. I had no desire to go down that road, fearing it would destroy my career which was just beginning to blossom. I had to face the harsh personal reality of paying the bills at home, with a wife in nursing school and student loans of my own to be paid. In essence, this became my dilemma, and mine alone. Struggling with the conflict of making a living or remaining true to what I knew to be the ethical path.

In addition, the faces of my nursing home clients haunted my thoughts. How I missed their company. The thought of the denial of quality mental health services for the confined elderly because of money profiteering schemes, became the deciding factor to report the wrongdoing.

At that moment I knew I had to do the right thing and report this to the State officials. However, I felt no great sense of relief. There was no uplifted feeling. I only felt great anxiety and fear as to what the future would hold for me. I felt like David taking on Goliath, without even the benefit of a slingshot. However, deep down, I knew that doing what is right and following your convictions is the best practice, even though there may be a high price to be paid. I hoped that enough public awareness would stem from this exposure, to prevent any further abuses in this area at this agency or others.

I began planning the action to be taken. First, I would take the Medicaid documentation home with me and review it all again to double check the incriminating facts. Then it became obvious that I needed others to support my claims and be willing to stick their necks out when things got rough.

The two people most knowledgeable of the history of the Geriatric Programs were Madelyn McGuire and Dick Hayes, my former supervisor. Both were Geriatric Supervisors with considerable work experience and were well-liked and respected by Agency staff. They also were aware of the lack of professional staff coverage problem, billing issues, and growing dependence of the Agency on the revenue generated by the Geriatric Programs. I met with both of them to discuss the Medicaid folder I had found. Dick confirmed that in the past, he was constantly pressured by the Executive Director to boost billings and hire more paraprofessional staff. He was uncomfortable with these demands, but felt his job and good standing with the Director, depended on his following through. He did what he could to try to stay in compliance with the Medicaid regulations.

Madelyn's regions of Geriatric Programs were run with a lack of professional coverage issues. She had hired several

B. A. level Social Workers' who were certified by the State to provide service in the nursing homes. However, she was aware of programs outside her domain that were pressured to cut corners and increase billings. Both were in agreement of the seriousness of the information I had discovered and agreed to substantiate these violations. It was determined that the Medicaid Fraud Unit with the State Office of the Attorney General would be the proper entity for notification. We believed the State Attorney General would be in a position to protect us from possible retaliation from the Agency, as the reporting "hotline" assured anonymity for anyone making a complaint. At the end of the meeting, I thanked them for their courage and support. I would be reporting this to the authorities and asked if I had their permission to use their names. Madelyn gave her permission with clear conviction in her voice. However, Dick seemed suddenly anxious, but agreed to go along with the reporting to the State. I began feeling better about the situation, knowing that both supervisors' would support my claims. I no longer felt totally alone and believed the State authorities would protect us from reprisals by the Agency. At least that's what I thought.

Two days later, following much soul searching and prayer, I called the State Medicaid Fraud Hotline to advise them of the possible fraudulent billings stemming from the alteration of Medicaid billing forms submitted by the Agency which had resulted in thousands of dollars in payment for improperly provided services.

About a week later, three individuals arrived at my office, presenting their identification from the Attorney General's Office. I provided them with the Medicaid folders and explained how they came to be in my possession. After taking a few minutes to scan the documents, they asked if I had actually delivered these services. I responded that I had not, stating that I had only personally provided a small number of these billed services. The vast majority were provided by paraprofessionals and the billing statements had been altered by deleting the paraprofessional code and replacing it with my professional billing code. The investigators appeared to be very interested in the initial findings and pledged to fully explore the incriminating documents. The investigation would include a full audit staff to review medical records and billing submissions. They asked for directions to the Agency's Executive Director's office, thanked me for the information, and said they would be back soon to interview staff. As they were leaving, I expressed concern for myself and others' willing to cooperate with their investigation and sought some assurance that we would be protected from Agency retaliation. The lead investigator stated that he hoped the Agency Director and the Board of Directors' would be motivated to cooperate and not interfere with the investigation or any participants involved. I hoped he was right, but somehow I knew it was time to prepare for the impending storm that was about to descend upon me.

Chapter III

Day of Reckoning

The day of reckoning arrived. On that morning, the Executive Director called me to advise that he had met with State investigators' regarding the Geriatric Programs and that the Agency was under investigation. He told me to report to his office the next morning at 8:00 am. Upon arrival for our meeting, I received a cool reception and his tone became increasingly confrontational. He wanted to know what I had told the investigators. I reminded him of the earlier problems we had with providing professional coverage in the nursing homes and that they had requested any written documentation regarding the Medicaid program.

I told him I had cooperated with the investigators' and gave them three files focusing on billings and correspondence between the Agency and Medicaid officials. He exploded! He told me I had no right to turn over internal papers to the State, that I should have refused to talk to them, and referred them to him. My response was that I assumed the Agency's policy was for all management staff to cooperate with the State by being forthright and honest with them. I told him once more, that for a long time I felt pressured by management staff to beef- up Medicaid billing by cutting corners in regard to compliance with Medicaid regulations. He was dismissive to what I said; stating loyalty to your employer was paramount and above all other things. He accused me of being ungrateful for all the opportunities he had given me. He proceeded to remind me that the promotions I had received were at his discretion and what a short memory I had. He ordered that I not speak to the investigators' should they contact me again, and refer them to him. I informed him that I was obligated to be cooperative and would not be involved in any cover-up or deception. My view being, that we should admit our actions; records were improperly changed, and repay any money received for the services in question. He brushed me off and again warned me not to speak with any State officials' or media.

I realized the trouble I was in with the Agency and knew there was no turning back. This was the point of no return. Oh, how I missed those earlier quiet days of just being a Therapist visiting a small town nursing home.

At this point the meeting ended, but I was informed that he would be calling a special meeting of the Board of Directors for that night. I asked if I was to attend, but he said "No". Later that day, he asked me to stop by his office. When I arrived, he seemed to be much calmer and even friendly in his tone. He began our encounter by apologizing for his earlier rudeness and said he believed this whole issue of improper billings was just an agency communication problem, which could be easily resolved.

He began blaming the whole state of confusion on Dick Hayes. According to his assessment, Dick misunderstood the State Medicaid regulations and became "loose cannon on the ship." He further complained that Dick was overly ambitious and reckless as a supervisor. He stated these were the reasons he had reassigned Dick to another program.

Again, he reminded me of how he had "taken me under his wing" and saw great potential in my abilities. He told me of an Executive Director position that would become available in another part of the State in about six months. He said with his help, I could be selected for this job. I listened, saying very little. Then he restated the importance of loyalty, and suggested I should express some confusion to the State about who was making the decisions about Medicaid regulations, and Dick appeared to be solely in charge of the day-to-day administration of the programs. His agenda was obvious to me. I assured him that I would report to the State my impressions of the events and would be totally truthful in doing so. I felt I had no other option, no matter where the chips eventually would fall.

At that point he abruptly jolted up from his chair, glaring at me and with a terse voice stated, "I don't want to hear any speeches from you!" He proceeded to tell me, "You're full of shit!" The impasse was obvious, I walked out.

The State Medicaid Fraud Unit investigative team descended upon the Agency during the next several weeks. Staff interviews were being conducted and documents were confiscated and sent to the State capital. The Executive Director was constantly badgering me regarding my disloyalty to the Agency. He also confronted the other two key staff for their apparent disloyalty to him and the Agency. However, because of my position as Associate Director, I had become the enemy and turncoat.

A smear campaign directed at me was initiated by the Executive Director. He constantly attacked my professional and personal character before my peers, other staff, and even with members of the Board of Directors. My office telephone records were audited for the previous two years. The long distance calls made to my home were cited as being telephone misuse. These were brief calls made to advise my family that I would be late coming home from work. I was required to repay the Agency for every call.

Local and statewide media coverage commenced and the Agency was assuring the public that no wrong doing had occurred and the three staff central to the investigation were "disgruntled employees" that had a "vendetta" against the Executive Director. All agency staff was instructed to not talk with the media and refer all inquiries to the Executive Director.

As the storm grew worse, the Geriatric Supervisor, Madelyn McGuire, received a telephone call from the Agency's previous Comptroller, who asked to meet with her. After work, Madelyn went to her home. The previous Comptroller told Madelyn she had read in the newspaper about the Medicaid fraud investigation. She took Madelyn outside to her parked car, opened the trunk, and retrieved a thick bundle of Medicaid documents. The documents were previously rejected billing statements regarding Geriatric Services.

The ex-Comptroller explained that just prior to her leaving the Agency; she had received these Medicaid billing rejections. Along with the rejections, was a letter from the Medicaid Division Supervisor, stating that these billed services were not delivered by a certified professional, and therefore out of compliance with the federal regulations. The Medicaid official also stated that the Agency had been notified several times earlier about this same violation and needed to correct this problem as soon as possible.

At that point, she gave Madelyn a second bundle of billing forms that were for the same dates of service, but altered with only professional codes. She said she had been ordered to resubmit these billings back to the State, which she admitted to doing earlier. However, this time she decided not to resubmit the billings, and hid them in the trunk of her car. Having already submitted her resignation, she knew she would be gone before the Accounting Department would notice the missing forms.

She told Madelyn that she felt these altered billing forms should be turned over to the State investigators'. However, as she was no longer an employee of the Agency, she did not believe it was her place to personally give them to the State. Madelyn took the documents and told her she would give them to her immediate supervisor.

The next morning, Madelyn came into my office with the documents and describe her meeting with the ex-Comptroller. After examining the forms, I could see that they were from the counties and nursing homes where I had previously been assigned. The billing forms had my professional code added, as well as the professional code of Dick Hayes. The next thing I needed to do was to check the medical record service date entries, in order to determine who had actually delivered the services.

The next day, I retrieved a sampling of the note entries and saw that the notes were typed and signed with only my signature or Dick's signature. These notes were a sample of the removal of the earlier handwritten notes, which were removed and replaced with the typed medical record entry. I turned the bundles of documents Madelyn had brought to me, over to the State investigators' for auditing purposes.

These weeks were hell. A line had been drawn. The Executive Director portrayed Madelyn, Dick, and me as the enemy who were attacking the Agency. He attempted to rally the Agency staff against us, even saying the investigation could result in the Agency being closed and everyone losing their job. If this happened, it was our fault! The retaliation continued at a frantic pace. I was followed by the Director and other staff in various vehicles during lunch breaks. We saw the writing on the wall. There was a major effort to discredit us and destroy our reputations and careers. We felt we had to secure legal representation.

Within a few days, we met with an attorney and explained our situation. We described how we had cooperated with an official State investigation into possible Medicaid fraud. This led to a chain of events of Agency retaliation measures against us, which included various forms of intimidation, public statements discrediting our reputation and character. We explained to the lawyer that we felt there was no other option but to be truthful and cooperative with the State investigation. The attorney said our Constitutional right to free speech was violated and recommended we file a suit in Federal Court against the Executive Director and the Agency's Board of Directors.

Shortly following the filing of the law suit, the media picked up on it, uncovering our claim of Agency retaliation against us for cooperating with the State Attorney General's Office. The Executive Director began taking administrative actions against me, changing my job title to "Planning Director" and moving me to a makeshift office which had previously been a staff break room located directly across from his office. His behavior toward me was intimidating and hostile each day.

I recall him singling me out at a group management meeting as being disloyal and a traitor to the Agency who paid my salary and had promoted me. My response to the entire group was there are some things more important than loyalty to your employer, such as God, family, and country. I also made the point that I was tired of these "office games" and to "go ahead and fire me". Everyone except the Executive Director suddenly became very quiet. He acted defiant, but did not act upon my suggestion. During this time media representatives were attempting to interview other Agency staff not in management positions. The Agency responded by implementing a "gag order" for all staff forbidding them to discuss the investigation with any media under the threat of being fired.

Manipulations within the Agency's power structure were being implemented. It was reported in a major statewide newspaper, that the Board of Directors Chairman had resigned from the Board to take a Department Head position with the Agency. He was a schoolteacher with no previous management experience. Now, rather than being in a position of authority over the Executive Director, he worked for him.

As the investigation and court case slowly moved forward, the daily badgering I endured finally reached a boiling point and I could take no more. I felt I was stripped of all personal rights and liberties for the eight hours I reported to work each day. I resigned from the Agency. The attorney used the legal term "constructive discharge", defining my resignation which resulted from "extreme pressure from the Agency".

Now I was unemployed, yet I still could not move on with my life. I felt I was at the abyss of my career. Unexpectedly, a ray of hope appeared. In an article published by a major newspaper, the subject of nationwide Medicaid fraud and abuse was highlighted. The United States Congress and President Jimmy Carter were making this issue a high priority.

Congressman Tim Lee Carter, of Kentucky; the only physician serving in Congress at the time, was a ranking member of a House Committee which had responsibility for funding mental health centers. It occurred to me to call his office and request a meeting with him when he would be in Kentucky.

I was very nervous about how slowly things were progressing. There was no movement on the State investigation. Kentucky politics and the connections the Executive Director had with a wide range of State Department Heads at the State capital worried me. It was impossible to know who to trust. The three of us who cooperated with the State investigators felt let down that they had done nothing to protect us from the retaliatory actions by the Agency. We believed they had an obligation to shield us from the Agency actions.

Madelyn and Dick continued to be harassed almost daily by the Director and other staff. Dick's wife, who worked in the Accounting Department, was verbally accosted by the Director for bringing a small space heater to use in her drafty office. He yelled at her about the cost of electricity and ordered her to turn it off and remove it from the premises. We complained to the Attorney General's Office regarding the mistreatment, but our complaints fell on deaf ears.

Personal attacks against Madelyn, Dick, and me accelerated. I was informed by a co-worker, that he had attended a staff party where rumors were circulating about inappropriate sexual misconduct between Madelyn and me, as well as with other women. This angered me, knowing how damaging this kind of gossip mongering could be for us, professionally and personally. Living in a small town, explosive rumors such as were being conjured up at this party, would surely spread throughout the Agency and then the community.

I did not wait long for my concerns to become reality. One day I was at a local nursing home, meeting with an elderly resident. In the middle of the counseling session with her, a man appeared at the door to her room. He abruptly interrupted our discussion, demanding to speak with me privately. He was obviously rude, and his demeanor was angry. He abruptly accused me of having an affair with his wife, Madelyn. I made it quite clear to him that this accusation was false, and he was out of line interfering with my counseling session, upsetting this elderly woman, and making a scene at the nursing home. He continued with threats and ranting of these ridiculous accusations. He departed, continuing to hurl threats as he walked out the door. I was left to apologize for this disturbance to not only the elderly lady I was counseling, but to several facility staff who were aroused by the disturbance which had been created.

Within a few days, rumors were circulating that the janitor had found ladies' undergarments in my office. I contacted the janitor, who denied having any knowledge of this rumor. I was furious! The deliberate attempts, by an unknown and cowardly person or persons, to concoct and spread these damaging lies, were having the desired affects. Madelyn was having serious problems with her husband, as a result, causing increasing stress and strain on her marriage.

I also felt the sting of these vicious rumors. Madelyn's husband contacted my wife, sharing the rumor that I was having an affair with his wife. Not only was Madelyn's husband a victim of these rumors, he became a perpetrator of the same lies victimizing other innocent parties. To this day, I regret the deep and irreversible damage these rumors caused so many innocent parties, and how their lives were ultimately affected.

Retaliation took a more direct approach as threats of physical violence played out for me. Upon returning to the office following lunch one day, I had received a large funeral wreath, complete with wilted, dead flowers, and a large black ribbon, which had been delivered by a local florist. The accompanying card read only, "With Deepest Sympathy." Promptly contacting the florist to find out who had sent me the wreath, I learned they had "no paperwork" identifying who had made the purchase. I was receiving prank telephone calls at my home.

The most serious act of personal violence occurred early one morning. It was still dark, the time of the morning as I traveled down the parkway that few trucks or cars were on the road. I was in the slow lane, going about sixty miles per hour, when suddenly I was hit from the rear with tremendous impact. The force of the collision sent my car rocketing off the parkway into a field. I was struggling to steer the vehicle so it would not flip over or hit a tree. Eventually, the car stopped in the middle of a cow pasture, about a thousand feet off the road. I was dazed, but not injured. The force of the impact knocked my glasses from my face into the back of the car onto the floor.

I was able to get out of the car and found the left rear panel and trunk had been crushed. There were tire tread markings on what was left of the trunk. Getting back into the car, I was able to get it started and it was still somewhat drivable. I got the car back onto the parkway and headed back to town. I looked for the offending vehicle, but nothing was there. There were no oncoming headlights in my mirror, no horn sounded prior to the impact. It was a hit and run incident. I thanked God that I was not injured and left out in that field. The car dealership assessed the damage, determining the car to be a total loss.

I now had serious concern for my safety. It was hard for me to believe that this was a deliberate attempt by someone to injure or kill me. No doubt, my involvement in the State investigation, along with the false sexual misconduct rumors, had resulted in persons who viewed me as the enemy. The intense hostility and anger directed toward me by my employer, coupled with the message inferred by the funeral wreath, and the threats of a jealous and irate husband, gave me reason to worry about my safety.

I considered reporting the incident to the police as a deliberate hit and run, but there was no concrete proof. It was time to demand some protection from the Attorney General's Office. The blatant string of harassing events directed at me, but also Madelyn and Dick, needed to stop! My complaints to the State Investigators' fell on deaf ears.

There was no question I was concerned about my own situation, but I also felt responsible for involving Madelyn and Dick into this tempest. The only recourse was to ask for Federal help. At that point, I knew I had to take a gamble with Congressman Carter. I made the call for an appointment.

In late November, 1979, Madelyn and I arrived at the home of Congressman Carter in Tompkinsville, Kentucky. The Congressman himself answered the door. In his office were a number of bookshelves filled with books and a massive desk cluttered with papers and two telephones. I explained that we were employees of the Mental Health Center located in his congressional district. I began telling him the entire story about how we cooperated with a Medicaid fraud investigation of our agency and were harassed and retaliated against by the Executive Director. We expressed concern that we were getting no protection from the State and had filed a Federal lawsuit against the Agency. Madelyn told the Congressman of her demotion and how I had been removed from my position as Associate Director. We were being portrayed as being disloyal to the Agency and responsible if the Agency had to close its doors.

Congressman Carter said he was aware of the pending Medicaid fraud investigation and knew of some prior problems with the center. He explained that he was on the House of Representatives Interstate and Foreign Commerce Committee which had jurisdiction over the Community Mental Health Centers'. He went on to say that he was appointed to a Special Commission on mental health issues by President Jimmy Carter. This bi-partisan commission was chaired by the First Lady, Rosalyn Carter. They were working, in conjunction with the Congress, to establish a new Mental Health Systems Act, which would be the new Federal Law drafting and implementing mental health funding and program services across the nation. He expressed his concern for the widespread fraud and waste of taxpayer funds within the Community Mental Health Centers and assured us that Congress would be addressing these issues directly. He asked if we were willing to go public with our complaints, stating he knew a reporter with a major newspaper who might be interested in doing an article about the matter. Agreeing to look into the situation, he placed a call to his Washington office, making various inquiries as we were sitting in his office.

He thanked us for helping to uncover improper activities and restated that Medicaid fraud was a major concern of his House Committee and that he took this matter very seriously. Our meeting concluded with Congressman Carter saying he would be in touch with us and we would be contacted by the newspaper.

We left the meeting with the Congressman feeling highly optimistic and recharged with new hope that some kind of intervention would be taking place shortly which would help us.

The following week, I received a telephone call from a reporter of the newspaper to schedule a meeting. At our first meeting, I went through the entire time I expressed concern that the nursing home elderly were a high risk group that often needed psychiatric services and they appeared to be neglected. The Agency placed more emphasis on billing Medicaid for large group arts and craft programs than span regarding the investigation, agency retaliations, and filing of the law suit. focusing on individualized one-on-one therapy sessions. In my view, income generation was promoted rather than quality of service and a "Medicaid mill" was in operation, with medical records being altered and false billings being submitted for thousands of dollars. At this point, I felt it was crucial not to hold back nothing; spell it out in detail, and backup everything I was saying. I was no trouble maker.

My work record at the agency was impeccable. I was hired as a line counselor and within just eighteen months became the Associate Director of the entire agency; this being an agency of four hundred employees with a five million dollar per year budget. Now the Executive Director is depicting me as unprofessional and a disgruntled employee. Just two months before the investigation of the Agency commenced, this same Executive Director gave me high marks on my annual employee evaluation and wrote that I was "a definite, valuable asset to the Agency."

I also stated for the record, that I did not seek the limelight or confrontation, but I was dealing with a chain of events that forced me into either covering up or exposing clear cut corruption. I was aware that there could be damage to my career, but I saw no other choice. At that point we felt that we were simply twisting in the wind with no positive resolution evident. We were drifting toward an abyss of personal destruction. Our earlier cooperation with the State investigation resulted only in harassment, retaliations, demotions, and slander of our reputations. However, changes were on the horizon awaiting us.

The day finally arrived regarding news from the State Capital. The Medicaid fraud investigation was completed. (See Kentucky Attorney General Final Report). The Attorney General's Office released investigation findings that the Agency falsified records and improperly billed the Medicaid program in the amount of several thousands of dollars. The Agency was ordered to pay back this money. The amount the Agency was ordered to pay back was only a fraction of the number of bills and records altered. The actual dollar amount of improper payment was never disclosed. However, no criminal prosecution would take place due to the fact that no individual received personal gain. Nevertheless, the Agency had to admit in writing that the improper alteration of documents had occurred.

Of course, we felt exonerated as our allegations had been confirmed. Naively, we hoped the Agency would now reverse their negative actions against us. We believed if they offered to restore us to our positions and good names, we would in turn consider dropping the suit against the Agency. How wrong we were. No relief was given.

The Agency abuse directed to us only got worse! The findings of wrong- doing, spelled out in the very public agreement the Agency had to admit to, and sign, only outraged them more. The second hammer to drop for the Agency, was taking place in Washington D.C.

The Congress was drafting new legislation regarding all mental health service programs nationwide. This new law would be known as "The Mental Health Systems Act." In the House of Representatives, the new law was being formulated through the House Committee process, and sponsored by a ranking committee member and the sole physician, Congressman Tim Lee Carter of Kentucky.

Congressman Carter was a powerful member of the Congress, highly respected and well-liked by fellow colleagues. He gained national attention in 1968, when then President Lyndon Johnson, appointed Congressman Carter to accompany eleven other congressional leaders to go to Vietnam to evaluate our war effort. He was the only member of the delegation to inform the President that in his opinion, we were losing the war. Not a popular assessment with the President, or Congressman Carter's own party, it demonstrated the great courage and statesmanship of the man.

At the Committee hearing in Washington, Congressman Carter introduced an amendment to the Mental Health Systems Act, called the "Whistleblower Protection Clause." The following is the direct exert from the House of Representatives Congressional Record, August 22, 1980: "Finally, Mr. Chairman, I would like to mention that the bill includes a requirement for any project receiving funds through The Mental Health Systems Act, to have in effect what is known as a "Whistle Blower" protection system.

Under this provision, any employee who reports a violation of State or Federal law or regulation may not be discriminated against with regard to his employment. This requirement, which I offered as an amendment, was based on an unfortunate experience in my own state where several employees were treated unfairly by a Center Director because of their truthful allegations.[1]

MENTAL HEALTH SYSTEMS ACT

Public Law 96-398 October 7, 1980

Pg. 1593-Sec (3)

Assurances that the applicant has in effect a system, satisfactory to the Secretary, to assure that an employee of the applicant who reports to any officer or employee of the Department of Health and Human Services or appropriate State authority, any failure on the part of the applicant to comply with an applicable requirement of the Act or regulation of the Secretary or requirement of State Law will not on account of such report be discharged or discriminated against with respect to the employee's compensation or terms, conditions, or privileges of the employee's employment."

Congressman Carter notified us of the amendment he was sponsoring and of the conference committee meeting with the Senate. The Senate committee Chairman was Senator Edward Kennedy, who indicated the committee's support of this Whistleblower Amendment for inclusion to the overall bill. Shortly after this, the new Mental Health Systems Act with the Whistleblower Protections was passed by the Congress and signed into law by President Jimmy Carter.[2] Those employee protections are still part of that law, some thirty years later.

Today, it gives me great satisfaction knowing that over these years, many other people may have been protected for following their convictions. Unfortunately it did not protect us.

For years after all this took place, I felt somewhat frustrated that my earlier actions of reporting wrongdoing and the resulting protection under the law, failed to protect me. However, I began to realize that feeling sorry for myself would not be productive and that a larger life lesson was taking shape. Suddenly it became clear to me that we were part of an event and set of chain reactions that brought to life the U. S. Constitution, in a very personal way.

For the first time in my life, the Constitution was real and not merely words in a history book. The Constitution is a living force. This living force began for us the day we walked into the Congressman's office. We were not a powerful special interest group or a well-connected community leader. That day in his home office, Congressman Carter saw young and scared mental health workers armed only with a principle. That key principle was the God given right of free speech. In short, protected speech regarding the reporting of wrongdoing and corruption of public funds. The Congressman must have noticed the almost child-like faith in our expressions of civil liberties and constitutional rights. However, I can say at the conclusion of the meeting, I somehow knew that our voice was heard.

Our forefathers declared certain inalienable rights were granted to us by our Creator. Freedom of Speech was the First Amendment framed in the Constitution as one of these key rights. The provision for whistleblower protections framed in the Mental Health Systems Act brought to life our Constitutional system of protections for all citizens. To be an eye witness to this modern day reaffirmation of long established civil liberties as formed in the whistleblower protection measures, remain a priceless gift to me. This special gift dwarfs any selfish and personal ambitions I may have had.

However, reality was still upon us. In addition to the humiliation the Agency felt as a result of admitting to wrongdoing and repayment of funds to the State, the newest public embarrassment was the media coverage of the Whistleblower clause in the Federal Law which originated due to the personnel abuses inflicted on the three Agency whistleblowers'. Our case resulted in a lot of media coverage on local television and through the major state newspapers. On three occasions, front page stories covered the Kentucky Attorney General's investigation and the resulting findings confirming the wrongdoing. Also, Congressman Tim Lee Carter's sponsorship of the Whistleblower Protection Amendment received extensive coverage.

The local Bowling Green, Kentucky newspaper, THE PARK CITY DAILY NEWS, ran the following front page article on Thursday, October 16, 1980:

JOB ACTION RESULTS IN NEW LAW

"A new mental health law signed by President Carter last week, contains provisions which are a direct result of alleged job harassment of three employees of the Barren River Comprehensive Care Center, according to U. S. Rep Tim Lee Carter (R Tompkinsville).

In an interview with radio station WKCT, Carter said the law includes a section prohibiting agencies which receive funds from the Department of Health and Human Services from discharging employees who report alleged non-compliance with state or federal regulations.

The "whistle-blowing" section of the law is based on the allegations of harassment made by three Comp. Care employees who provided information in a Medicaid-Medicare investigation.

Comp. Care employees Richard Hayes, Madelyn McGuire, and William Marohnic have filed a federal civil rights suit in connection with the alleged harassment.

Carter also told WKCT that a federal investigation into claims by the three employees that they were instructed to alter records at the Comp. Care center has determined the allegations were true."[3]

Coverage of the Board of Directors' Chairman resigning form the citizen board to take a high level management position with the Agency without experience or qualifications, while the scandal was taking place, was also suspect. At that point, the only thing rendering us some protection was the Federal lawsuit we had filed against the Agency several months ago.

The legal machinery moved slowly with depositions and evidence gathering. Of course the Agency continued to claim innocence, proclaiming to be the victims of "a few disgruntled employees." Meanwhile, talks started to take place with the attorneys representing both sides, regarding possible settlement.

Going to court always involved some risk and we all wanted closure. I wanted to put an end to this and move on with my life. Having submitted my resignation, I was unemployed. Madelyn and Dick were still with the Agency, but isolated from others and singled out as traitors.

We believed we had been a success with the whistleblower protections built into the law, but still very uncertain about our professional futures. We were grateful to our families, friends, and others who had offered support through this ordeal. However, it was obvious no reforms or changes would be made at the Agency, so we had no choice but to move on.

In the end, we settled the suit. Two major reasons prompted this decision. The stress was having a negative impact on Dick's health and Madelyn's husband was giving her a lot of grief about her involvement in the lawsuit, as he had friends on the Board of Directors. The second reason involved what we believed to be a pattern of poor advice and direction form our lawyer.

In the settlement agreement, Madelyn and Dick were required submit their resignations from the Agency. We all received what amounted to a year's salary and a positive written reference letter from the Executive Director for us to use in seeking new employment. The Agency did not have to admit to any wrong doing. It was not a great deal for us, but at least put an end to it all.

A couple of weeks later, we met at the lawyer's office to settle our legal bill. We received the written letters of recommendation, and the settlement checks. Saying "good-by," Madelyn, Dick, and I, went our separate ways. It was a bitter-sweet day for me. I felt we had been wrongly punished and "run out of town", while the main offenders remained untouched and gainfully employed. Even with the Agency admissions of fraud and the Congressional reform legislation, which was a result of this one agency's Executive Director's retaliatory actions, we were worn down. At least we had the satisfaction of knowing what we had to endure could not happen to others who would act on their convictions.

As we departed the lawyer's office that cold winter day, I was so grateful to embark on a new direction in my life and to leave this Agency and its Director behind. Little did I know that they were not through with me yet!

Chapter IV

Whistleblower's Curse

This was the beginning of a new life for me. Even though no reforms were made at the Agency, I felt exonerated by the successful completion of the fraud investigation and the new whistleblower protections enacted by Congress. I had a positive letter of recommendation form the Agency, and in addition, my employment record was impressive. As Associate Director, I supervised approximately two hundred employees, including clinical, administrative and clerical staff. My resume included very positive work evaluations and record of three major promotions within eighteen months. I was certain I would find fulfilling employment at a level near the position I held at the Agency.

There was a surplus of job opportunities available to those with experience and a Master's Degree in Social Work, so I began sending out my resume. Before long, I started receiving promising responses. I began getting phone calls from interested employers', who voiced their intention of getting back to me to arrange for a job interview. However, I would never hear from them again.

This pattern of initial high interest and no further response became more evident as the weeks and then months passed. There was one job possibility that looked very promising. I was even scheduled for an interview. During the meeting, the interviewer stated that I was very qualified for the position and he was eager to hire me, but needed to call my former Executive Director for a final recommendation check. I was ushered to a waiting area.

In a few minutes, I was recalled to his office. He told me I was overly qualified for the position and he had to withdraw his offer. I became very suspicious. I contacted another potential employer who also had gone suddenly cold, and he recommended that I not use that letter of recommendation from my prior employer. It was hard for me to believe the Barren River Mental Health Board, and its Executive Director, my former boss, would somehow sabotage my efforts to secure employment, especially since the positive letter of recommendation was ordered by the court as a part of the settlement agreement. I needed some proof that the Agency's Director was violating the court order.

Bob Craig was a lifelong friend of mine and lived in another state. I decided to ask Bob for his help. My plan was for Bob to contact my former Executive Director, posing as an interested employer considering hiring me. Bob agreed to help me with this plan, and in a few days made the phone call. Bob asked my former boss, the Executive Director, for his employment assessment of me. According to Bob, the assessment given was not positive. Without saying so outright, the comments made by my former boss were very suggestive that Bob, my perspective employer, should not consider hiring me.

I was outraged! I now knew why I was not able to find work even after sending out seventy applications over a two year time frame. In my mind, this was a fragrant violation of the Federal Court Order which mandated the Agency to issue positive employment references.

Although my wife was gainfully employed as a registered nurse, I was not able to further contribute to the family finances. The earlier court settlement funds were depleted. It was a dismal situation for my family. I became very depressed and fearful as to what the future would be for me. I realized that my former employer was out to make certain that I would never again work in my chosen profession. By this time, I was unemployed for three years and rapidly becoming unemployable because of the long break in my employment history. I was again facing an abyss of personal destruction.

I had to pursue legal redress. I contacted a small town lawyer with a well-known reputation for taking on lost causes. He was a country lawyer with principles and integrity. He was familiar with my earlier case and knew of the reputation of the Agency and its Executive Director. He agreed to take the case on a contingency basis, with the condition that I would assist him as sort of a legal aide. I would help him research case law that would be applicable to my situation.

The case was filed in U.S. District Court, with the complaint outlining the violations of First Amendment rights, coupled to the breaching of the earlier court order mandating positive work references. The Agency's response to our legal complaint was that they had honored the Court's order by providing the written positive letter of recommendation; however, they were not obligated to provide any "verbal" statements, which would substantiate the court ordered written letter.

It was blatantly evident to me, that the Agency circumventing its own official written positive letter of recommendation with unofficial verbal negative references, given to my perspective employers, was intended to sabotage all employment opportunities for me, and nullified the Court order. Without question, this attitude demonstrated outright malice and bad faith by the Agency's Director. Beyond the malice, this struck me as showing a lack of honor. Not honoring the spirit of the Court order, and stating this action publicly as a legitimate legal defense before a Federal Judge, is incredulous.

A few months later, the District Court dismissed the complaint by Summary Judgment for the Defendants, the rationale being I did not establish damages. I was devastated by this ruling. I could not understand how the Judge could find that I did not establish damages! The Agency had successfully blocked me from obtaining employment each and every time I was being seriously considered for hire by interested employers.

The Court dismissal of my suit left me at a dark place without any hope to salvage my career. I felt I was at the end of my rope. I had no employment prospects and I appeared to be at the mercy of the Agency who already has deprived me for three years, from obtaining a job.

After the District Court ruling came down dismissing my case, I met with my attorney, Tom Noe. He discussed the need to file an appeal to the Sixth Circuit Court of Appeals. This court was one step below the U. S. Supreme Court. He would argue my case in front of the judges of the Court of Appeals. He stressed the importance of legal research and put me to work that very day. My job was to research in the U.S. Code Law Books for any Civil Rights cases that were focusing on First Amendment issues. Whistleblower cases were the preference. We proceeded with an appeal of the lower court ruling with the Sixth Circuit Court of Appeals in Cincinnati, Ohio.

I began spending day long sessions at the local university Law Library looking for cases that were similar to mine. Unfortunately, I could not find many cases that fit the legal framework we needed for the appeal. My attorney was also researching several cases which could support our argument.

I was becoming increasingly frustrated in my search attempts. We had a court date for my attorney to present his argument before the court. Time was running short. I had found a couple of cases which might be helpful. Finally, following weeks of research, I found a case quite similar to mine with a favorable court ruling. I was grateful to find this case. My attorney was pleased as well.

My personal situation was as grim as my employment prospects. My finances were at rock bottom. The bills kept piling up and the debt collectors were showing up at my doorstep. It was very humiliating and frustrating for me to have to face my family and friends under these circumstances. At this point, I felt completely alone and shaken regarding my beliefs and the values I upheld, which led me to this abyss.

The only haven I had left was my faith. I was not normally a praying man, but during these challenging times I prayed a lot. God does answer prayers. Not always in a way we fully understand, but in His way.

I moved my family to a rented house on a large farm in the country. My landlord was a successful big-time farmer who owned and operated several thousand acres. He was well known throughout Kentucky, having won the Farmer of the Year Award several times. He also operated a large country ham business. People called him Haz, and he became my mentor and my friend.

Haz patiently taught me some of the basics of working with the land. I began growing a garden and was surprised at how rewarding this labor was for me. However, I was still facing an indefinite and unresolved future.

In addition to cultivating a very large vegetable and flower garden, I started raising chickens, ducks and geese. Eventually, my gardening evolved into truck farming, which helped supplement the family income. With direction from Haz, I embarked upon small scale livestock farming, which also contributed funds to the family. My two children were teenagers and enjoyed participating in this new farming life.

After what seemed an eternity, my lawyer argued the merits of my case before the Appellate Court. The Defendant's lawyer did not attend the oral argument. September of that year, we received notice from the Court of Appeals that they reversed and remanded the District Court ruling and ordered legal proceedings to move forward.

A lengthy written argument was composed by the Chief Justice in which he stated, "We hold therefore that Marohnic's speech which exposed graft and corruption in government touched upon a matter of public concern. Next, Marohnic's speech in this case no way hindered the operation of The Board. Rather, Marohnic's speech increased The Board's efficiency by helping to disclose the fraudulent altering of bills. Marohnic's speech to the Kentucky Attorney General's investigators concerned fraudulent billing by The Board. Public interest is near its zenith when ensuring that public organizations are being operated in accordance with the law. Public policy strongly supports and encourages protecting speech at the behest of law enforcement officials. This context further reveals that Marohnic's speech was induced by civic commitment, not by an employment related dispute." C Pg. 616-800 Federal Reporter, 2nd Series.[4]

In closing, the Court ruled, "Since we hold that Marohnic's speech was protected by the First Amendment and that material issues of fact exist concerning both whether Walker made negative statements about Marohnic's qualifications and Walker's motivation for doing so, we reverse and remand this case for further proceedings." C Pg. 617-800 Federal Reporter, 2nd Series.[5]

The day I received the written copy of the Appellate Court ruling, is a day I will always remember. Joy and relief swept through me like a bursting dam. My prayers were answered! The system worked! I was vindicated!

My children were old enough to comprehend the words and the meaning of the court ruling. Over the years, they had witnessed first-hand, how their father struggled with the repercussions of his speaking out. The resulting impact of that decision was direct and personal for them, and probably made them question the merits of getting involved or taking risks. The court ruling confirmed that justice can prevail. It did for their father. I very much regret; however, that their lives were impacted in any negative way, by decisions I had made.

Also, during those many difficult years, I regret the burden placed upon my wife of having to be the main family breadwinner. To her credit, she never complained, and showed great courage and resolution as she pursued in her own right, a distinguished career in nursing.

Shortly after the Appellate Court ruling, the Agency contacted my attorney about settling the case. They offered a large enough amount of money for me to start over. Certainly not enough to retire, but enough to pay some bills and finally begin anew. If we proceeded to Court, things could be tied up for years. I was too mentally exhausted to pursue this any further.

Reviewing the entire episode form day one, I concluded that much was accomplished. From a personal point of view, I realized my career in the mental health field was over. Too much time had passed for me to be employable. I was totally spent and reluctant to get involved the bureaucratic jungle and rat race.

I will always remember my two associates during the early years. Madelyn and Dick had moved on to successful and rewarding careers. I was happy for them. The Agency identified me as "the ring leader" and targeted me for several more years.

I am not bitter or angry for what happened to me, and I have forgiven the

Agency's Executive Director who put me and my family through so much Hell. On the day I settled with the Agency at the lawyer's office, the Executive Director, who at the time was on medical leave, approached me at a moment when we were in the room alone and apologized for his actions over the years. I believed he was sincere, and I let go of any remaining resentment; grateful to be free of the dark emotionally exhausting shackles of the past years.

From a larger perspective beyond the small framework of my life, I see a greater good has resulted. In essence, this saga is not really about one individual. The events transcend the players involved and become more relevant to those who would follow us. The added protections for new whistleblowers' hopefully will spare them the crushing hardships imposed by menacing employers who would be out to silencing any uncovering of corruption.

The Marohnic v. Walker case has clearly highlighted free speech protections for whistleblowers. These First Amendment case law findings, from the Appellate Court ruling, have been heavily referenced by many on-going Free Speech cases. No doubt, beneficial outcomes and relief will be afforded through the Courts to those persecuted for exercising their Constitutional rights. The light of free speech will always illuminate the darkness that spawns graft and corruption.

Chapter V

For the Record:
Road to Redemption

Whistle blowing can be defined as an act of reporting wrongdoing within an organization to internal or external bodies.[9] Also, the act of reporting wrong doing may or may not be protected speech. First Amendment speech protections rendered by Federal Courts must meet several guidelines.

This criteria should involve public or government employees and pertain to reported violations falling within the realm of public interest or concern.[160] Workplace internal grievances closely aligned with job performance or lack of, do not fall within the scope of protected speech. Overall, personnel and labor arbitrations, also do not qualify for First Amendment protections.

In addition, reporting of wrongdoing must be weighed or balanced against the degree of damage or harm it inflicts on the organization.

My case was cited in a recent U. S. Supreme Court case, "When an employee exposes unscrupulous behavior in the workplace, his interests are co-extensive with those of his employer; both want the organization to function in a proper manner." Marohnic v Walker, 800 F 2nd 613, 616 (6th Cir. 1986)[171] Therefore, any contemplation of becoming a whistleblower must be exercised with caution and serious thought.

In my case, I was very fortunate to meet the legal guidelines for Federal protections. To begin with, I was a public employee, working for a government funded agency. Also, my reporting of wrongdoing did not relate to internal labor grievances. My whistle blowing focused on potential Medicaid fraud, as well as abuse of public funds. These allegations were reported to the Kentucky Attorney General's Fraud Unit, which was an external body.

The Federal Court ruled that my cooperation with the State investigation was a matter of public concern. The court also stated, "public interest is near its zenith when ensuring that public organizations are being operated in accordance with the law." Marohnic v Walker 800 F.2nd 613, 616 (6th Cir. 1986). In short, I was very fortunate in meeting the requirements for First Amendment protections. Most whistle blowers are not so lucky. Unfortunately, only 29% of non-profit organizations have whistleblower policies that provide employees guidelines and protections when they go public in reporting violations.

For the record, my personal journey as a whistleblower has led me over time, down many roads. Some were smooth, others were rock-strewn. Over time, they would transverse into a career nexus encompassing two milestones. The first milestone was the Whistleblower Protection Clause included in the Mental Health Systems Act of 1980. The second milestone was the Marohnic v. Walker Federal lawsuit in 1986. Both of these events were triggered by the reporting of wrongdoing during the Kentucky Attorney General's Medicaid fraud investigation in 1979.

My role was only being the trigger that set into motion a sequence of events which involved the contributions of many people and their labors. Key institutions, such as the Congress and Federal Courts were instrumental in shaping the final outcomes.

The whistleblower protections were advocated by the late Congressman Tim Lee Carter. He chose to use our example of three young mental health workers' who reported Medicaid fraud in his Congressional District. His steadfast sponsoring of applicable whistleblower protections became law in 1980.

A few months earlier at a Congressional Hearing, Congressman Carter stated, "For the record Mr. Chairman, the Whistleblower Amendment adds a new requirement to the list of conditions which an applicant must fulfill in order to receive funding under this legislation.

Specifically, the Amendment requires the applicant to have in effect a system, satisfactory to the Secretary of Health and Human Services, which assures that any employee who reports a failure on the part of the applicant to comply with State or Federal law or regulation, will not be discriminated against with respect to his compensation, or the terms, conditions, or privileges of his employment. Mr. Chairman, the need for this Amendment grows out of a recent experience in my State in which three employees of a Mental Health Center reported substantial violations of State regulations with regard to the Center's billing procedures. As a result of this report, an investigation is now underway, but the employees have suffered significant hardships according to their reports. One employee has effectively been demoted, another resigned in anticipation of being fired.

I would hope that with the Amendment I am proposing, that future violations of law and regulation can be reported without fear of reprisal from employers'. I regret that such a requirement is even necessary, but I believe it is. We must do all we can to promote efficient operation of these Centers' and in return we should protect employees from future unjust reprisals." (Committee of Interstate and Foreign Commerce-Passed U. S. House of Representatives, August 22, 1980).[182]

I am proud to be associated with this Amendment which affords employee protection for those that report corruption in their workplace. As a whistleblower, my journey led me down a road upon which I had no idea of the ultimate reach and scope. As mentioned earlier, my role was quite limited, acting only as a trigger by reporting wrongdoing and cooperating with the investigators.

These features merit some analysis. Congressman Tim Lee Carter was the driving force that made things happen. He took a local scandal regarding the misuse of public funds, and transformed the small scale dust-up to national legislative reforms that were dynamic and effectively designed.

To begin with, the Amendment has two enforcement components that give teeth to its application. First, the requirement for all applicants receiving funding to have in place a "system" to protect those reporting violations. This system has to be submitted to, and approved by, the Secretary of Health and Human Services at the time of application for funding. This mandates a link between funding and employee protection compliance. This should predispose the applicant employer to an awareness, and the importance of constructing and enforcing whistleblower protection safeguards. Thus, incorporating whistleblower protection systems as an enhancement to comply with and maintain critical funding requirements, makes the proposition far more likely to succeed over mere altruistic intentions absent the force of law.

Secondly, employee awareness of personnel policies that define protections for those reporting employer misconduct, should promote improved agency efficiency and communications, thus reducing the possibility of employer-employee strife and the need for whistleblower action. Another key area where the employee whistleblower protections have a positive impact is on client or patient care. After all, the ultimate goal is to provide the best degree of quality, regarding the delivery of mental health services.

As a whistleblower, I can only relate my experiences as a Social Worker in the Community Mental Health Center environment. In my own work experience, there was a constant battle regarding limited resources versus increasing income generation. Quality of care hinged on distribution of resources and the ethical commitment of the caregiver. Temptations were ever present to cut corners and reallocate resources away from patient care in order to fund pet projects. This becomes fertile ground for fraud, waste, and abuse. In my experience, two major infractions grew worse in terms of intensity and frequency. The quality of care diminished gradually reaching a sub-par level, while patient billing for services ever increased. This condition could be ignored only for a short time among conscientious caregivers.

During that time no policy existed for whistleblower protections. This concept was non-existent and would never be promoted by management. However, if the Agency had been required to formulate a personnel policy protecting employees who reported violations, in order to participate in receiving public funds, the day-to-day operations would have been improved considerably. Treatment delivery would be less exposed to cutting corners and the watering down of services. The adherence to regulatory compliance would be less likely to be compromised. These positive forces would naturally encourage improved quality of care and increase caregiver morale.

Congressman Carter's employee protection reforms were designed to shed light in previously dark areas. These affirmative changes could only promote the effectiveness and efficiency of the delivery of mental health services nationwide. In the final analysis, these reforms are designed to protect the rights of the whistleblowers'. This new law would in effect, discourage not only employer retaliation, but also the corruption which would facilitate the need to report.

As a Social Worker, I also can see the major benefits derived from improving treatment delivery. The reduction of waste, abuse, and fraud, will result in redirecting limited resources for client services. On a national level, and in human terms, the benefits would be vast.

My career journey also led me down a second rocky road which also reached a career nexus approaching a second milestone. The sequence of events began when I secured the legal services of a small town country lawyer named Tom Noe III, of Russellville, Kentucky. His quaint office was located in a historical building near the Court House square. I had met Tom earlier, when near the end of the case he was called on by our lawyer, to act as a second attorney in our original Federal lawsuit against the

Agency. I recalled that he was well-spoken, articulate, and most importantly, very professional with a code of ethics he wore on his sleeve. He had a special interest in Constitutional Law and was quite competent in areas of civil liberties. So six years later, I approached him, hoping he would agree to take my case against my former Executive Director and the Board.

Today, I consider myself very fortunate that he agreed to represent me in a case that eventually led to his oral argument presentation before the Sixth Circuit Court of Appeals, in Cincinnati, Ohio. From a legal perspective, for an attorney, it is a great experience to argue a case before a Federal Appellate Court, just a step below the U. S. Supreme Court.

Tom's diligence and determination with my case resulted in a dramatic victory and a stirring written opinion by the Chief Justice of the court. Over a quarter of a century, this court ruling in Marohnic v. Walker has become heavily cited First Amendment case law, throughout the country, even being quoted for employers to validate the discharge of employees. People are dependent on their jobs because they need their income, their health care and other benefits accessible with employment.

One of the most dominant restrictions on individual freedom is the power of insurance, their economic security for retirement.[13] This hold employers have on their staff can in certain situations, become tyrannical. In my situation, the wrath of retaliation was relentless. Daily harassment, badgering, and even veiled personal threats against me occurred with regularity. When I reported to work, it seemed I left my civil liberties at the front door and reclaimed them at the end of the day. In addition, the fear of being fired and the loss of income, kept me in a state of anxiety and constant state of uncertainty.

We all, under normal conditions, take for granted our basic freedoms. I was no different, until quite abruptly my civil liberties eroded at the hand of my employer. During the years I was searching for employment, the constant rollercoaster pattern of raised expectations and hope, followed by abrupt job denial, was agonizing and extremely frustrating. The range and intensity of employer retaliation extended over several years, inflicting continuous damage.

In doing case law research for this book, I am heartened in learning of the importance the Marohnic v. Walker case has had with many Federal Appellate Court rulings across the country. Others reporting wrongdoing, have become victims of the same predictable pattern of employer retaliation. They also sought judicial remedy for their unfortunate circumstance, and in many cases prevailed. They too, found deliverance from subjugation through the courts, and began the journey back to becoming whole once more.

Also in doing my research, I came to appreciate how attorneys and courts rely on prior case law to bolster their own legal arguments and decisions. Legal themes are either strengthened or weakened by selected case law already on the books.

The hallmark of my case was First Amendment Speech Protections which promoted public concern and civic commitment. In addition to court rulings, several legal journals and articles have touched on the core themes my case encompassed. "Speech concerning fraud and misuse of government funds during a Medicaid fraud investigation was found to touch upon a matter of public concern." Another law publication cited my case and stated a common theme used in many case arguments, "Public interest is near its zenith when ensuring that public organizations are being operated in accordance with the law…and seeing that public funds are not purloined." Wilkins v. Jakeway 94-4137 (6th Cir. 1996). The same case stated, "In Marohnic it found that the plaintiff's participation in the Medicaid fraud investigation did not hinder the Board's efficient operation but rather, improved it."[194]

I titled this chapter, "**For the Record**", to encapsulate what benefits or tangible results I believe came from my whistleblower journey. I did not plan my career as a Social Worker to follow a path of being a crusader. I was expecting to enjoy a long, fruitful, and fulfilling professional career experience, which would culminate in a peaceful and comfortable retirement.

I would never have thought I would be a good candidate to take on the standard of a whistleblower. I consider myself to be somewhat introverted and shy. I have never been one who seeks the limelight or embraces risky behavior. So, what happened?

Although the time I actually worked as a Social Worker was very limited, and my life has followed other vocations, I remain a Social Worker at heart. This was my true calling and where, I believe, I have made a contribution to humanity. As a Social Worker, I tried to do the right thing by remaining true to some basic convictions. As I reflect upon my journey, the bottom line is, WHAT A LIFE EXPERIENCE I HAVE HAD!!

In the beginning, three mental health workers, by reporting wrong doing, triggered a chain of events which involved powerful people, and through their actions, institutions that orchestrated vast changes for the greater good of society. These same people and institutions protected and delivered us from certain catastrophe at the hand of a vengeful employer.

Six years later, I faced the very same vengeful employer, but this time alone. The ravaging effects of years of blackballing and unemployment, came to a head when I sought legal redress with the hope of finally putting an end to this long nightmare. The legal showdown ended at the Federal Court Appellate level. This time, I was protected and delivered from catastrophe by the U. S. Constitution.

Little did I know when I cooperated with the Medicaid fraud investigators, my words and actions would impact my life so dramatically. The statements made years earlier were used against me in terms of unjust reprisals. Eventually, the very same words protected me and ushered in my deliverance, when the Federal Court declared the words to be protected speech.

Chapter VI

Rippling Waves:
Cast a stone upon the waters

The title of this chapter, **Rippling Waves**, has a poetic symbolism that associates the circles of waves emanating outward from a turbulence created by a stone splash upon the surface of a body of water. Using one's imagination, the earlier chapters focusing on the whistle blowing events, can be our stone splash; an event that created much turbulence to the previous calm of the water. More importantly, the book's introductory chapters lead the reader through a metamorphosis from an isolated reporting of wrongdoing, to the inception of newly formed public policy on a National stage, both within the Legislative and Judicial Branches of Government.

On the Legislative side, the whistle blowing event resulted in the "Whistleblower Protection Amendment" inserted into the newly created Mental Health Systems Act of 1980. The Amendment became a new Public Policy requiring all federally funded Mental Health programs to establish and enforce personnel policies protecting all employees who report wrongdoing from employer retaliation.

On the Judicial side, the metamorphosis resulted in the Federal Appellate Court ruling, "Marohnic v. Walker" which has garnered a twenty-five year track record emanating Public Policy framed as First Amendment Constitutional safeguards still heavily cited in contemporary litigations.

The question today can be asked, how relevant is this twenty-five year old Court ruling presently? Are there "rippling waves" emanating outward from the earlier stone splash which caused so much turbulence?

Here, the Author has capsulated for the reader, a composite of real life stories that pinpoint both the legal conflicts and the adjudicated resolutions that ultimately changed lives forever. These case studies will not be a dry legalistic review, but rather a humanistic and moving portrayal of individual profiles of courage resulting in personal and legal victories for those who placed themselves at great risk.

Each individual anecdote captures acts of personal courage risking careers, financial security, as well as professional reputations, all for personal conviction and workplace ethics. The foretelling of great personal sacrifice for the greater good captures the human spirit near its zenith, at the same time inspiring the reader by showcasing that honor and character still exist.

Also, these profile stories highlight the hallmark of innermost faith exhibited by every character in the Constitutional promise of Civil Liberties, reaching its own apex with each story's deliverance of protections and safeguards for those most at risk.

Lastly, the Marohnic v. Walker case is a good example of a 1986 Court ruling casting a long legal shadow. Hallmark to the case being Freedom of Speech safeguards, which touched and influenced personal lives in each of the Court cases presented spanning over twenty-five years.

In the final analysis, the sum total of the "Profiles of Courage" cases shared, in concert with each other, all have realized and achieved the "promise of the First Amendment" crafted so long ago by our Founding Fathers.

PROFILES IN COURAGE

In our first case, the Plaintiff, a former Chief of Ohio's Community Services, within the Department of Development, sued three Supervisors' alleging that he was wrongfully terminated from his job because he exercised his right of Freedom of Speech. The Court stated that the Plaintiff pleaded facts that if true, were sufficient to show that his speech was clearly protected.

The Plaintiff, Terry J. Wilkins, was formerly employed by the Ohio State Department of Development, responsible for monitoring agencies that receive Federal and State funds to help the needy. Wilkins job duty was to insure that the agencies complied with State and Federal regulations governing the allocation of funds.

In late 1993, the Plaintiff filed a Civil Rights law suit, stating that he had been fired in retaliation for his right of Free Speech. He alleged that he reported Agency misuse of State and Federal funds to his Supervisors' and to the Ohio Inspector General's Office. The Plaintiff further alleges, that his Supervisors' had threatened his welfare and his job because of his reporting of wrongdoing. They eventually fired him for said reporting. Wilkins further alleges that their actions were intentional, reckless and malicious. Additional stated claims of violations of State whistle blowing statutes, claiming intentional inflictions of emotional stress.

Wilkins claimed that he became aware of misuse of Federal funds in violation of Federal regulations, and of the fact the Department employees' had not corrected apparent violations. He reported the problems to the Defendants' and urged other Program Administrators', such as the Home Energy Assistance Program, to stop funding certain agencies. The Plaintiff alleged he was harassed for reporting the violations, and the Agencies' knowledge of them, that he received a Written Reprimand for discussing sensitive matters.

Also, Wilkins claimed he always followed the internal procedures to stop funding, and that his actions led to pursue decertification of one Agency after serious abuses were discovered.

Finally, he alleged that he acted as a concerned public citizen, not because of a conflict with his Supervisors'.

The Court stated matters of Public Concern include misusing of Public Funds, unethical or illegal practices in office or corruption. In the Marohnic case, this Court permitted a Social Worker for a State Board of Mental Health to bring a First Amendment suit against his employer who had forced him to resign by harassing him after he cooperated with a Medicaid fraud investigation. This Court found that Marohnic's speech concerning possible fraudulent billing was Constitutionally protected. The Court wrote that Public interest is near its zenith when ensuring that Public organizations are being operated in accordance with the law, and seeing that Public funds are not purloined. The Marohnic case also affirmed that speech charging corruption or discrimination is a matter of public concern, whereas speech complaining about incompetent management is not.

In this case, Wilkin's speech relates to a matter of Public concern. We must next balance the Plaintiff's interest in the effectiveness and efficiency of the office. Moreover, when the Court is engaged in this balancing test in Marohnic, found that the Plaintiff's participation in the Medicaid fraud investigation did not hinder the Board's efficient operation, but rather improved it. The Court considered the exposure of fraud always to be in the interest of the Government. The Court also noted that the working environment was not so intimate of such and interpersonal nature that Marohnic's cooperation…..rendered him ineffective.

In this case, the Court must balance the Plaintiff's interest in his speech against Ohio's interest in the efficiency of this Agency. Given the importance of speaking out against misuse of Public funds, the Plaintiff's interest is great. As we stated in Marohnic; when an employee exposes unscrupulous behavior in the workplace, his interests are co-extensive with those of his employer; both want the organization to function in a proper manner. The disruption that the Plaintiff caused by his comments at staff meetings clearly does not outweigh his interest in speaking out on this subject. The result of the balancing test in this case should be clear to any reasonable Government employee. Because of the above reasons we rule in favor of the Plaintiff and so order further proceedings.[1105]

In our second story, Clyde Conway as Plaintiff was hired in 1982, by the city of Kansas City as an electrical inspector. According to the Plaintiff's complaint, several work related problems occurred during a two year period. The first problem began when he was ordered by his immediate Supervisor to perform certain campaign work for the city's Mayor. Other problems developed when the Plaintiff refused to approve sub-standard electrical work for certain community development projects. Finally, the Plaintiff made public charges against his Supervisors' for ordering him to perform electrical work during City time on their homes and the homes of friends and relatives, sometimes without the proper permits.

The events which led to the Plaintiff's dismissal began in May, 1984. The Plaintiff was ordered to perform an electrical inspection of the Highland Park baseball field. During the inspection, he found several electrical violations which were a danger to the public. He refused to approve the Facility and submitted his report to his Supervisor. The Supervisor did not order the corrections needed and approved the Facility to become operational. The Plaintiff being aware of this action, prepared a written report concerning the violations which also criticized his Supervisor for releasing the Facility, even with the danger it posed to the public. He submitted the report to the Department Head and the City Administrator.

On the following day, the Plaintiff's Supervisor called him into his office and requested him to sign a letter of reprimand outlining various past episodes of misconduct and insubordination by the Plaintiff. Conway, refused to sign the reprimand, and tore it up into pieces and left the office. That same day, the Plaintiff's Supervisor prepared a memorandum recommending the Plaintiff's termination for failure to follow instructions and insubordination for tearing up the letter of reprimand. The termination was approved by the City Administrator on June 14, 1984.

After a formal grievance hearing, a Board of Review affirmed Conway's discharge based on insubordination. In a later hearing, a Referee for the State of Kansas, Department of Human Resources, reviewed the denial of unemployment benefits by the Plaintiff's former employer after hearing the testimony, the Referee found Conway's discharge did not demonstrate a breach of duty owed to the employer, and further found a lack of any willful intent on the part of Conway to go against the authority of his Supervisor. He therefore ruled that Conway was eligible for the unemployment benefits.

Thereafter, Conway filed a complaint against the city of Kansas City for violating his Constitutional Rights by wrongful termination. Conway asserts a First Amendment claim, alleging the City fired him NOT for the stated reason of insubordination, but in retaliation for his criticism of his Supervisor's actions. Conway argues several work related incidents contributed to the Defendant's decision to terminate him. To begin, Conway made public comments concerning work he was asked to perform on City time for City Officials', their friends and relatives, often without the required work permits and license. Conway claims he reported the questionable activities to the City Administrator and to the media, who questioned him on the subject.

In addition, the Plaintiff reported a certain amount of activities by his Supervisor which might have indicated illegal payoffs or kickbacks. Finally, Conway argues his termination was directly related to his criticism of his Supervisor. A week before his termination, Conway sent a written report to higher-ups' advising them that the Plaintiff's Supervisor had overruled his decision to reject the electrical work at the Highland Park baseball fields. Conway claims he wrote the report out of concern for public health and safety. The Court stated that speech which discloses any evidence of public corruption, impropriety, or malfeasance of the part of City Officials, in terms of content, clearly concerns matters of public interest, as cited in our Marohnic case.

The Court also focused on the motive of the speaker in analyzing whether the speech qualifies as a matter of public concern; i.e., whether the speech was calculated to disclose misconduct or dealt with only personal disputes and grievances with no relevance to the public interest. Conway public statements of potential wrongdoing did not focus on internal policies relevant only to Department personnel nor involve essentially a private matter, but concerned information in which the public would definitely be interested. Nor was Conway's speech motivated solely by personal interest or hostility, but was primarily for the purpose of informing his supervisors" of what he perceived to be improper and illegal conduct. Conway attempted to inform his superiors that the Building Inspections Department was not properly discharging its governmental duties. Conway reported facts to his superiors that appeared to involve special favors for Government Officials', illegal payoffs and circumstances of released substandard electrical work which he felt, posed danger to the public. In short, Conway sought to bring to light actual potential wrongdoing or breach of public trust on the part of a public officer. The Plaintiff has demonstrated his speech was that of public concern and therefore protected. The Plaintiff has prevailed and further Court proceedings are ordered.[1116]

In our next story, Everett Perry was hired by the Michigan Department of Corrections as an Administrative Law Examiner. Specifically, he worked for the Office of Policy and Hearings as a Hearing Officer and decision maker in major misconduct disciplinary hearings in Michigan State Prisons. On November 5, 1993, Perry was fired.

Perry filed his complaint, March 7, 1996. In part, his claim cited First Amendment violations. Perry asserts he was deprived of his First Amendment right to freedom of expression in two areas, (1) he suffered retaliatory termination because of his findings made as a Hearing Officer in prison misconduct hearings. (2) He suffered retaliatory termination because of his complaints of race discrimination.

We must determine whether Perry's decisions made in inmate disciplinary hearings constitute expression as protected by the First Amendment. We find that they do. We find that disciplinary hearing decisions fall within the scope of First Amendment protection. The Court also has deemed that retaliation by a Government employer against a person who exercises his First Amendment rights constitutes a First Amendment violation. The Supreme Court has established a three prong test for assessing whether a Plaintiff can prevail on a First Amendment retaliatory discharge claim under the test. The Plaintiff must prevail in three areas: (1) Speech must involve a matter of public concern; (2) The interest of the employee in commenting upon matters of public concern, outweighs the employer's interest in promoting efficiency of operation; (3) That the speech was a motivating factor in the denial of the benefit that was sought.

Here, the Plaintiff argues that he was fair and impartial in his disposition of disciplinary cases, and that each of his rulings was a communicative act protected by the First Amendment. He further alleges that by terminating him for that expression, his former employer infringed upon his freedom of expression. Perry also argues that for the first year and six months of employment, he received positive Supervisory evaluations. During the next twenty seven months, Perry only received four citations regarding his hearing rulings. However, the rate at which Perry ruled, NOT GUILTY with dismissal, was higher than the norm. His NOT GUILTY dismissal rate was between 17% and 18%. This rate was well above the norm of 10%. Soon after his Supervisors' noticed his higher dismissal NOT GUILTY rate, the frequency with which they cited him for substandard disposition of cases increased dramatically. After a revision of his case dispositions, his Supervisors assessed the Plaintiffs was prone to finding prisoners NOT GUILTY. Shortly later, the Plaintiff received the first of nineteen citations from his Supervisor over the next sixteen months, pointing out mistakes in his disposition of cases. Perry's colleagues during the same time period made many of the same mistakes, but were never cited. The Plaintiff was terminated two weeks after receiving the last of the nineteen citations.

The Court assumed that Perry's decisions in inmate hearings constitute matters of public concern. When Perry conducts hearings, he is doing so at the behest of the Michigan Legislature, and is making decisions that can result in a greater or lesser period of incarceration for the inmates. These are intensely public matters.

Furthermore, the public has an interest in a public employee's efforts to remain undeterred by a public employer's policy that seeks to limit constitutionally mandated fairness in inmate disciplinary hearings. In Marohnic v. Walker A case in which the Court examined what constitutes a matter of public concern, the Court concluded that public interest is near its zenith when ensuring that public organizations are being operated in accordance with the law. Public interest is certainly near its zenith here.

The Plaintiff asserts that through his disciplinary hearings decisions made with an eye toward justice and impartiality, he was ensuring, at least to the extent of cases which he was responsible, that the Michigan Department of Corrections was operating in accordance with the law.

The Court believed that there were institutional pressures to reduce the NOT GUILTY dismissal rate throughout the prison system. The Court stated at the very least, expectations that the dismissal NOT GUILTY rate not rise above 10%. The prison officials believed NOT GUILTY rates above 10% raised a red flag. If hearing officers maintain a 90% guilty rate, they cannot possibly maintain impartiality as it is required to be in accordance with the law. Because Perry's speech served to ensure that the prison system, an arm of the State, was operating in accordance with the law, it concerns the most public of matters.

Therefore, the Plaintiff prevailed and the Court ordered further proceedings.[1127]

In our next profile, Plaintiff Carolyn T. Rogers brought this Civil Rights suit claiming the Defendant wrongfully terminated the Plaintiff from her employment in violation of her First Amendment right to free speech. The Court ruled the Plaintiff produced sufficient evidence of a First Amendment retaliation claim.

The Plaintiff was employed by the Pauline Warfield Lewis Center, an Ohio State Mental Hospital in Cincinnati. She began her duties as a Social Worker and was eventually promoted to Director of Quality Management, a position created to prepare the hospital for surveys by the Joint Commission of Accreditation of Hospitals, (JCAH), and other survey organizations. The Plaintiff reported to Alice Gray, Director of Support Services, and Gray reported to the Defendant. On January 21, 1999, the Defendant revoked the Plaintiff's unclassified appointment. In a memo informing the Plaintiff of the revocation, the Defendant stated, "I no longer have confidence in your ability to function as the Quality Management Director, your verbal and written communications are not conducive to a cooperative work environment."

Specifically, the dispute centered on various statements the Plaintiff made during her tenure at the hospital. In citing one example, the Defendant maintained the Plaintiff's manner and method of communications had offended and inflamed her coworkers at the hospital. There was an incident where the Defendant authorized relocating a staff member's office to a location which was used by the patients. The Plaintiff sent a memo to the Defendant claiming the relocation of the office would compromise patient privacy and possibly raise issues during the next JCAH survey. The Plaintiff alleged during a mock survey, she was amazed to see that a patient program/visiting area had been altered into an MD's office unit. She also stated that this set a precedence for other MD's to have special needs that rationalize taking large patient and visiting areas for office space. In short, the patient's needs, including space for visits with families as well as privacy for visiting, should be the most important factor.

According to the Defendant, other communications, considered to be unprofessional included: (1) Arguing with the Housekeeping Director about the cleanliness of the restrooms in front of other staff, (2) Arguing with other staff and then detailing the incident in and e-mail to the Hospital Director, (3) Presenting a Quality Management report at a staff meeting in a "very angry and hostile manner", and accusing management staff of not caring about quality standards. The Plaintiff admits to these communications, but contest the manner and disruptive nature of her statements as described by the Defendant.

The Plaintiff filed an amended complaint alleging that the Defendant wrongfully terminated her for exercising her First Amendment right to free speech.

The Plaintiff in her claim focuses heavily on the concern for quality patient care. In August of 1998, a memo by the Plaintiff described its purpose of "Survey Preparedness" as well as "Patient Rights and Ethics". The memo further explained that the hospital would be subject to an upcoming JCAH survey and that the last survey conducted at the hospital found a deficiency regarding patient privacy. The Court believed the Plaintiff's point, as we review the memo's content was to call the Defendant's attention to what the Plaintiff perceived as a disregard of patient privacy at the hospital, not to complain about management or other internal disputes. Therefore, drawing all reasonable inferences from the evidence, we hold that the Plaintiff has established the threshold requirement that the contents of her August 17, 1998 memo addresses a matter of public concern.

We now must consider whether the employee's memo and comments interfered with the performance of her duties on the job. Did her comments undermine the legitimate goals of the employer? Did they create disharmony among the staff or impair discipline by Superiors, or destroy the relationship of loyalty and trust of employees?

The Defendant argues that the Plaintiff's memo was disruptive, inflammatory, and interfered with working relationships at the hospital, and therefore the facility's interest in promoting its efficiency outweighed the Plaintiff's First Amendment interests. We first note that the Plaintiff's memo, on the surface, does not appear to be inflammatory. The memo is critical of the Defendant's decision to use patient space for doctor's offices. No abusive language is evident and we do not indicate any insulating language.

In our case, Marohnic v. Walker, <u>when an employee exposes unscrupulous behavior in the workplace, his interests are</u>

co-extensive with those of his employer, both want the organization to function in proper manner.

Furthermore, the Defendant presented no evidence that the Plaintiff's memo disrupted the hospital operation or efficient functioning. In short, the Defendant has not shown a State interest that outweighs the Plaintiff's First Amendment rights to call the Defendant's attention to the quality of the hospital's patient care.

Therefore, we order further proceedings regarding this case.[1138]

In this next story, the Plaintiff, a former public employee, filed an action against her former county agency and general county officials alleging that she was terminated in retaliation for her statements to State investigators' exploring possible misconduct in the county agency.

The Plaintiff, Deborah Hudson, began working for the Washington County Juvenile Service Office in 1984, first as a volunteer and then as a Secretary in 1985. She was elevated to the rank of Juvenile Court Officer, as it was titled at the time of her discharge in 1990. It was during an investigation of her Supervisor, by the Tennessee Bureau of Investigation (TBI), and Hudson's involvement in that investigation, which she alleges precipitated her discharge.

The TBI began its investigation of her Supervisor after a former employee of the Juvenile Service Office publicly questioned the conduct of the Supervisor while in office. According to the Plaintiff, she was then contacted by the TBI and she complied with their request that she give a truthful statement regarding her Supervisor's behavior while in office. Hudson shared with the TBI her observations of her Supervisor, which included misappropriated funds and equipment, falsified time records and mileage logs, and improperly handled checks and money orders. Hudson never publicly discussed these charges with the press or any other public body.

The Supervisor subsequently resigned from office in 1990, as part of an agreement with the District Attorney that charges against Stuart would not be pursued any further in return for his resignation.

After her Supervisor's resignation, Defendant Stanley was promoted to Director of Juvenile Services, which was under the jurisdiction of the Washington County Juvenile Court and Judges Stewart Cannon and John Kiener, both who are Defendants in this action. The Plaintiff alleges that when Stanley, Cannon, and keener became aware of her cooperation with the TBI investigation, they harassed and threatened her. Specifically, Stanley told Hudson, she did not want to work with a "NARC", and that she intended to go after those who made statements against the former Supervisor, and that she would "take care of" those who cooperated with the investigation. Judge keener allegedly told Hudson that "he'd better not find out" that the Plaintiff had cooperated in the investigation. All these statements occurred prior to her Supervisor's dismissal.

The Plaintiff alleges that the harassment and retaliation continued. Her job duties were reduced. Summaries of staff meetings were not distributed to her and her desk was moved to a back store office, so she had less contact with the entire office. In addition, Stanley complained about the Plaintiff's work habits, despite her excellent work record, compiled prior to the TBI investigation. Finally, in August, 1990, she was fired by Judges Cannon and Kiener, who controlled personnel decisions in the office.

The Defendants claim that several legitimate reasons exist for Hudson's termination which does not complicate the First Amendment, according to the Defendants. The Plaintiff's accusations destroyed the harmony in the office and disrupted staff relations. Her alleged insubordination, lack of professionalism, absenteeism, failure to take responsibilities, lack of creativity, and lack of a college degree, all contributed to her termination.

The Court ruled that the Plaintiff's allegations do concern speech which was a matter of public concern....Speech disclosing public corruption is a matter of public interest and therefore deserves Constitutional protection, and this form of alleged disloyalty does not affect the proper functioning, properly due to malfeasance.

At the time of the Plaintiff's termination, the general contours of public employees' First Amendment rights were clear. Speech of a public employee is protected if the speech addresses a matter of public concern. In Marohnic v. Walker, Plaintiff's cooperation with a Kentucky Attorney General's investigation resulting in an admission of fraudulent billing, but in no interference with the operation of the Agency, was protected under the First Amendment.

Therefore, we must decide whether the Defendant's reasonably could have believed that the harm to the efficiency outweighed the Plaintiff's interest in speaking freely. Again, in Marohnic, when an employee exposes unscrupulous behavior in the workplace, his interests are co-extensive with those of his employer; both want the organization to function in a proper manner.

The Plaintiff's speech which highlights public corruption and therefore deserves Constitutional protections and other speech which outweighed governmental concerns for efficiency.

The propriety of Hudson's discharge centers on the factual question of whether the Defendants had proper motives for their actions. In order to establish First Amendment violations, the Plaintiff must demonstrate that her protected conduct motivated the Defendant's action. In closing, we affirm and decide in favor of the Plaintiff and order further proceedings.[1149]

In the case of Plaintiff Hetzel D. See v. Defendant Chief Michael Medders, the Plaintiff See brought an action as a police officer against Chief of Police Medders for a First Amendment violation of rights when disciplinary actions were taken against the Plaintiff after he made statements to the FBI about activities in the Police Department. The Plaintiff was hired as a patrol officer for the city of the Elyria Police Department in 1993. He was also a member of the Police Officer's Union and served as Union President from November 1999 to January 2003.

The Plaintiff's complaint stems from a disciplinary action taken against the Plaintiff for violations of various Police Department rules and regulations. The Plaintiff contends that the actions taken against him were for and in retaliation for the following exercise of his First Amendment rights: (1) Statements he made in 2001 newspaper articles criticizing Chief Medders, and (2) statements he made to the FBI regarding allegedly corrupt activities within the city's Police Department. The Plaintiff contacted the FBI to report immoral activities within the Department.

Charges were brought against the Plaintiff by the Police Department regarding rules violations, as well as insubordination. He was suspended for fifteen days. The Plaintiff was also accused of failure to perform his duties as an evidence technician. The Defendant recommended that the Plaintiff be terminated. After a disciplinary hearing, he was terminated on April 2, 2002. After a disciplinary hearing in November, 2002, an Arbitrator reduced the termination to a thirty day suspension. The Plaintiff was reinstated on December 2, 2002.

On October 2, 2003, the Plaintiff filed suit against the City and Chief of Police Medders for First Amendment violations. These violations were based on his being disciplined in retaliation for the Plaintiff's Union activities and speech in matters of public concern.

The Plaintiff alleges that the Defendant violated his First Amendment rights by discharging him in retaliation for making statements to the FBI regarding alleged wrongdoing in the City's Police Department. The Plaintiff must establish the speech was protected. He must show his statements were of public concern. He must also show his speech demonstrated that his interest in the speech outweighs the Government's interest in promoting the efficiency of the public service it provides as an employer

If the speech issue is found to be a matter of public concern, this Court must then determine whether the Plaintiff's First Amendment interest outweighs the Defendant's interest in promoting the efficiency of the public service. The Court also states the truthfulness of the employee's statements is not relevant in determining whether the speech involves a matter of public concern unless, of course, the employee intentionally or recklessly made false statements, then the truthfulness of such statements may be relevant as one factor striking the relevant balance between the employee's rights to free speech and the employer's interest in efficient administration.

In Marohnic v. Walker, <u>Public interest is near its' zenith when ensuring that public organizations are being operated in accordance with the law....</u> The perception of potential graft and corruption is deserving of vigilant protection by the First Amendment. The public has a vital interest in the integrity of those commissioned to enforce the law.

In balancing the interests, we conclude that the City's interests in promoting the efficiency of the public services it provides does not sufficiently outweigh the First Amendment right to disclose allegations of misconduct within the Department to the FBI. Other than Medder's own statement to another officer, that an FBI investigation would affect Police Department morale, there is no evidence that the Plaintiff's complaints to the FBI actually impeded the Police Department's general performance and operation, or affected loyalty and confidence necessary to the Department's proper functioning.

The Court ruled the Plaintiff's speech to the FBI was of public concern and did not hinder the proper operation of the Department, and therefore is protected by the First Amendment. The Plaintiff prevails on these grounds, and therefore further proceedings are ordered by the Court.[2150]

In the following case profile, Plaintiff Paul Hatfield joined the Sheriff's Department as a Deputy in 1986. Plaintiff Fred McCoy joined the Department in 1987. Both Plaintiffs' were promoted to the position of Investigator in March of 1988, and to the rank of Detective, the highest rank for a Deputy Sheriff in Pike County, Kentucky, in February, 1989.

Both Plaintiffs' observed practices in the Sheriff's Department that they defined as corrupt and illegal. In November of 1987, they started expressing their concerns to the FBI. Eventually, the Plaintiff's went public with their accusations. They held a press conference where they presented their complaints. The Plaintiff's described the Sheriff's Department as a small mafia, with the Sheriff as the Godfather.

The Plaintiffs' charged that the Sheriff directed his Deputies not to serve Bench Warrants on people with whom he had personal or political ties. Deputy Hatfield detailed seven instances in which the Sheriff told him not to serve Bench Warrants. Other Deputies supported these claims. Several Deputies testified they Th were asked by the Sheriff to hold Warrants from being served. Sheriff Keesee denied ever holding up Warrants from being served. Other Deputies in the Department supported the Sheriff's position. Sheriff Keesee was also accused of fixing drunken driving arrests.

According to the Plaintiffs', several Deputy Sheriffs' in the Department had felony convictions. The Sheriff fired the Deputies three days after the press conference at which the charges were made. The Sheriff cited "conduct calculated to disrupt the orderly and effective operation of the Sheriff's Office". The Plaintiffs' filed their suit in August of 1990. Relying on the First Amendment, they sought reinstatement to their jobs and compensatory and punitive damages. Perhaps the most important factor for the Court to consider is the object of the speech. In Marohnic v. Walker, <u>Public interest is near its zenith when ensuring that public organizations are being operated in accordance with the law.</u>

The Court has also held that speech disclosing corruption is a matter of public interest and therefore deserves Constitutional protections. Obviously, the public is concerned how a Police Department is operated, and efforts to give the public exposure to alleged misconduct is protected.

Subsequently, the Court ruled the Plaintiff's speech was a matter of public interest and therefore protected by the First Amendment.[2161]

In the next circumstance, Odis Solomon joined the Royal Oak Township Police Department in 1966 as a patrolman. He received several promotions during his employment and served as Public Safety Director, also known as Chief of Police, from 1974-1978. While Director, the Plaintiff investigated acts of corruption by employees of the Department and members of the Township

Board of Trustees. In 1981, the Plaintiff was again named Public Safety Director and continued to investigate the allegations of corrupt behavior by Township employees. Sometime in the spring, a Board member informed the Township Mayor that the Plaintiff had raped a female police officer. Other allegations were made that the Plaintiff had sexually molested three Department employees. Michigan State Police were called in to investigate the charges. The Michigan State Police investigation concluded, with no charges filed against the Plaintiff. However, no clear resolution became of the matter and subsequently, the Plaintiff was replaced and removed from his position and demoted to patrolman.

On several occasions, the Plaintiff was interviewed by the press, at which time he stated his innocence regarding all allegations made against him. Later, he was warned by his Supervisors that he would be fired if he made any further statements to the press. He obeyed this order, but a radio station broadcasted his earlier written statements. The Plaintiff was fired on April 26, 1985. The Plaintiff's complaint claimed violations of his First Amendment rights to freedom of speech.

The Court has decided that a State cannot condition public employment on a basis that infringes upon the employee's constitutionally protected interests in freedom of expression. Our task is to seek a balance between the interest of the employee as a citizen, in commenting upon matters of public concern and the interest of the State, as an employer, in promoting the efficiency of the public service it performs through its employees.

Marohnic, again is cited, <u>Public interest is near its zenith when ensuring that public organizations ate being operated in accordance with the law.</u> Expression of public issues has always rested on the highest rung of the hierarchy of First Amendment values. Speech concerning public affairs is more than self-expression. It is the essence of self-government. A police officer's perception of potential graft and corruption are deserving of vigilant protection by the First Amendment.

Subsequently, we affirm that the Plaintiff's speech was protected and we order further proceedings.[2172]

The next case involves a civil rights action for retaliation against the exercise of free speech by a public employee. Dale Hoover was employed in the Circleville, Ohio Building Department as a Building and Electrical Inspector. The current action stems for Hoover's public statements criticizing the Department while he was an employee. During the course of his employment, Hoover argued with his Supervisor over the proper procedures to be used in inspecting buildings. Soon after the disagreements became concrete, the Plaintiff's Supervisor instructed him to approve several building permits to placate him. The Plaintiff found several violations which he could not overlook. In another building site, the Plaintiff found that the building was built without a permit or drawing. Hoover also found numerous code violations, including several fire hazards. The Plaintiff gave the owner's ninety days to correct the violations and refused to grant a permit until the violations were corrected. The Plaintiff's Supervisor issued a certificate of occupancy without any corrections made.

As a result of this incident, the Plaintiff began to voice his concerns publicly. Hoover spoke to the Building Department's Advisory Board, which is made up of local builders', about the improper practices. The Plaintiff also contacted the State Chief Plumbing Inspector, to inform him of the Department's efforts to conceal all the violations. The Plaintiff also went to the city-wide Supervisors' Meeting, intending to raise his concerns. The meeting was a closed forum and he was asked to leave. Hoover was later disciplined for attempting to attend the meeting.

Both Supervisors' warned the Plaintiff to stop discussing the Building Department and ordered him to stop publicly discussing the fact that he had been ordered to approve non-compliant projects. The Supervisors' told Hoover it was not appropriate to "spill bad news all over the community". The Plaintiff was warned that his job was in jeopardy if he continued to criticize the Department in public.

Two months later, the Plaintiff and his Supervisor had a physical altercation. Hoover was copying some papers in preparing to file suit against the Building Department and his Supervisor.

The two argued with some shoving and verbal threats exchanged. Shortly later, Hoover was given notice of a disciplinary hearing. He did not attend the hearing because he could not arrange for having an attorney present. However, the Plaintiff was terminated for the following reasons: (1) Refusal to carry out work assignments, (2) Assaulting his Supervisor, (3) Intimidating language to his Supervisor, and (4) Conducting personal work during business hours.

Hoover brought his civil rights action, claiming the Defendants' violated his First Amendment speech rights.

Hoover has stated a claim of First Amendment violations regarding free speech. When public employees' allege that he was terminated in retaliation for protected speech, we look for the following, (1) Speech is protected if it is a matter of public concern, (2) The speech must be of sufficient importance to outweigh the interest of the State.

In this case, Hoover's speech included informing State Officials and CitizenBoards about the improper procedures being used by the Building Department. When of that institution is a matter of public concern.an institution oversees some aspect of public safety, the correct cooperation

The Court ruled that the interest in public safety outweighs the State's interest in conducting its affairs. Termination is an adverse action that would chill speech in a person of ordinary firmness. We must also look at the Defendant's motivation in terminating the Plaintiff. In Marohnic v. Walker, <u>An act taken in retaliation for the exercise of Constitutionally protected rights is actionable.</u>

Also, the Plaintiff was disciplined for attempting to speak in public about the actions of the Department. Hoover was censured for attempting to attend the Supervisors' Meeting. He was warned that his job would be in jeopardy if he continued to discuss in public the Department's failure to comply with the law. The Plaintiff's termination notice stated that he had been fired for refusing to carry out work assignments. Some of these work assignments wee those that he had been ordered to approve; had refused and had then discussed publicly.

We affirm that the Plaintiff's speaking out regarding matters of public safety are protected and we order further proceedings.[2183]

In the next unique case, Julia Ward as Plaintiff alleges that Eastern Michigan University (EMU) fired the Plaintiff from the University's Graduate Counseling Program due to her religious beliefs of the subject of homosexuality, in violation of the First Amendment.

EMU Counseling Graduate Student, Julia Ward, filed the complaint in 2009, alleging the EMU Board of Regents violated the Plaintiff's First Amendment free speech and religious rights. The EMU Counseling Program prohibits Counselors from advising clients during a counseling practicum course, that they should refrain from homosexual conduct. The Plaintiff alleges that EMU required her to affirm or validate homosexual behavior.

The controversy arose when Ward's third client sought counseling regarding a homosexual relationship. After reading the file, and about one hour before meeting the client, she asked her Supervisor whether she should refer the client to another Counselor, because she could not affirm the client's homosexual behavior. At that point, the Supervisor informed the Plaintiff she would not be assigned any more clients, and that the Supervisor would be requesting an informal disciplinary hearing. The Supervisor believed the Plaintiff may have violated EMU's policies set forth in the Counseling Student Handbook.

The Handbook states of prohibits unprofessional conduct or an inability to tolerate different points of view, or imposing values that are inconsistent in counseling goals and discriminatory based on sexual orientation. After a disciplinary hearing reviewed the set of circumstances leading up to the hearing, they, on March 2, 2009, informed the Plaintiff that the panel unanimously concluded that the Plaintiff be dismissed from EMU's Counseling Program. The panel assessed that Ward violated the code of ethics...avoid imposing values that are inconsistent with counseling goals. Counselors do not condone or engage in discrimination based on age, culture, or sexual orientation. Also, your own testimony indicates you are unwilling to change this behavior.

The Plaintiff argues in her action, that she was retaliated against for expressing religious beliefs, and that the Defendants' took action that would "chill the First Amendment rights of the ordinary person". A retaliation claim requires proof that the Plaintiff engaged in protected speech, adverse action was taken against the Plaintiff that would deter a person of ordinary firmness from continuing to engage in that conduct. Also, a causal connection showing the adverse action was motivated by the Plaintiff's protected conduct.

The Court must decide whether the reasons given for her discharge by the formal review panel were academically legitimate or were instead, a mere pretext to retaliate against Ward for expressing her religious beliefs.

The Court states that the Plaintiff's alleged conduct of asking whether she should refer the homosexual client to another Student Counselor, before she even met the client, and more importantly before the client met her, could reasonably be found to be consistent with the ACA code of ethics and the course textbook. Ward avoided imposing her religious beliefs on the homosexual client by asking for a referral to another Counselor. Ward explained that she did not ask whether she should refer the client because of his status as a homosexual, but because she could not counsel him concerning his homosexual relationship. The EMU Defendant's true motivations for dismissing Ward from the Counseling Program raise a factual issue of intent for which dismissal of the case or Summary Judgment is particularly inappropriate., Marohnic v. Walker.

Ward has sufficiently plead and come forward with evidence that EMU Defendant's act of dismissing Ward violated her First Amendment rights.[2194]

In this story, Carolyn T. Modica began working as an Inspector for the Texas Cosmetology Commission (TCC) in Beaumont, Texas, in August, 1990. The Plaintiff raised concerns for her Supervisor's demotion of her, and aired her concerns at a TCC meeting.

According to the Plaintiff, following the TCC meeting, her Supervisor's ignored and retaliated against her in various ways for voicing her concerns. The Plaintiff claims she was denied a merit raise and her application for a promotion was

In September of 2001, she was again denied a merit pay raise. In May, 2002, Modica sent a letter to a Texas State Senator accusing the TCC of (1) Cheating on numbers to make performance levels higher, (2) Eliminating the tracking systems of complaints, (3) Abusing travel expenses, (4) Misusing State funds, and (5) Permitting inappropriate activities in the workplace.

In March, 2002, she applied for the Executive Director position, but was turned down. Increased patterns of retaliation occurred, according to the Plaintiff. On September, 2003, The TCC terminated her employment and stated that no further positions would be open for her consideration. Modica subsequently filed a wrongful termination suit in retaliation for exercising her First Amendment rights. The suit was filed against the TCC and her Supervisor.

The Defendant's argued that the Plaintiff's speech was not protected because it did not raise a matter of public concern. The Defendant's also argued that her speech concerned private matters relating to personal employer-employee disputes. Although certain aspects of the Plaintiff's accusations involved employer-employee relations, the main content of the Plaintiff's charges were public in nature.

In Marohnic v. Walker, Public interest is near its zenith when ensuring that public organizations are operating in accordance with the law. The Plaintiff's choice to inform a public official outside the TCC, makes her speech public. The content of Modica's speech also favors protection. Although there is evidence of an employer-employee dispute, the majority of the Plaintiff's concerns did not relate to matters relating to her job, but to the operation of the TCC , as a whole. Modica expressed concerns regarding the elimination of the complaint tracking system, the delay in holding administrative hearings and the failure of the agency to distribute regulation books for which it received payment. Nor did the Plaintiff's charges focus on her failure to receive promotions or raises. The Plaintiff argued that her complaints urged that the public and the TCC deserves to have better representation, not that she receive a particular redress.

Modica's charges brought forth in the public letter, constitutes an effort to bring public attention to problems in the TCC administration of its public duties.

The Plaintiff also cited her concerns for misuse of State funds, not personal grievances. Indeed, it is not until after she made these complaints to the TCC that she alleges she was retaliated against by way of not receiving promotions. In short, we conclude that the contexts of her complaints are more public than private in nature.

Despite the presence of some private interests, the content, form and context of the Plaintiff's charges demonstrate that her speech is predominately public.

The Court also concluded that the Plaintiff's interest in commenting on these matters outweighed the Defendant's interest in promoting efficiency. The Defendant does not dispute the First Amendment's bar against retaliation for protected speech was clearly established Federal law.

For our purposes, the Court ruled that the Plaintiff's speaking out pinpointing alleged abuses and misuse of public funds, constitute an issue of public concern and further constitutes First Amendment protections for the Plaintiff. Thus, the Court also orders further proceedings in this case.[2205]

The next story should be interesting to the reader. This case involves the termination of Plaintiff Julie Pucci from her administrative position in the Nineteenth District Court, a Court within Michigan's Judicial System. The Plaintiff, Pucci, brought suit against both the Court and Mark Somners, the Court's Chief Judge, at the time of the Plaintiff's termination. The Plaintiff claims she was terminated in retaliation for her complaints to State

Court officials about Somner's use of religious language from the Bench, in violation of her right to free speech.

Julie Pucci began working at the District Court as a Court typist in 1991. She was promoted to Probation Officer in 1991, Judicial Aide in 1992, Clerk of the Court in 1994, and Assistant Court Administrator in 1995. The last position was reclassified in 1998 as Deputy Court Administrator, and the Plaintiff held this position until she was terminated in 2006.

Initially, Pucci worked as a Deputy Court Administrator without incident and received good employment evaluations. In 2004, however, she lodged a complaint with her Supervisor, the Court Administrator, regarding Somner's "practice of interjecting his personal religious beliefs into Judicial proceedings and the business of the Court." She also complained to the Regional Court Administrator and to the State Court Administrative Officer (SCAO), which oversees the administration of Michigan's Courts. Pucci was not alone in complaining. Sharon Langen, the Clerk of the Court, also testified that she complained to the SCAO, and another Court employee filed a complaint with the State Judicial Tenure Commission. Judge Foran, also stated that he received upwards of fifteen complaints from local attorneys' about Somners interjecting his religious beliefs from the Vench or imposing sentences based on religion.

Pucci was being considered for the Court Administrator position. The Plaintiff was well-liked and respected by all the staff. However, Somners' objected to the Plaintiff's planned promotion, arguing that she and another Court Judge's romantic relationship created an inherent conflict.

Somners' began to lobby for the Plaintiff's termination as a Court employee. Eventually she was demoted because of her involvement with a sitting Judge and violating ant nepotism rules of the Michigan Court System. She would serve as Deputy Court Administrator.

On January 1, 2006, Somners' became Chief District Judge. Coinciding with his elevation to Chief Judge, Somners' began to evaluate the performance of the Administrative staff.

On October 10, 2006, Somners' reorganized the administrative Court Structure and eliminated the Deputy Court Administrator position. On January 1, 2007, Pucci would be terminated.

The Plaintiff has testified that Somners' told her that her termination was due to her relationship with Judge Hultgreen, and not due to budgetary concerns. Somner claims she was fired because of dissatisfaction with her job performance. Prior Chief Judge Foran testified that he thought Somners' terminated Pucci for personal reasons and because of her unmarried relationship.

On February 12, 2007, Pucci filed suit against Somners'. the District Court, and the City of Dearborn. She filed the complaint primarily under the First Amendment retaliation clause as well as the Whistleblower Protection Act. The nature of Pucci's complaints implicates the propriety and legality of public in-Court Judicial conduct, renders her speech of sufficient public gravity and warrants First Amendment protections. Again, in Marohnic v. Walker, Public policy is strongly expressed, "Public interest is near its zenith when ensuring that public organizations are being operated in accordance with the law." If the Plaintiff shows that the speech at issue addresses a matter of public concern, the Court must also consider whether the employer had an overriding State interest in effective public service that would be undermined by the speech.

The law governing First Amendment retaliation claims has been well developed. The facts of the case's retaliation claim dovetail with her successful First Amendment claims, where a Plaintiff was terminated because he or she publicly disclosed serious and often constitutional misconduct by Superiors. At the time of the Plaintiff's complaints, the law had clearly established that her comments were constitutionally protected as a matter of public concern, and that termination in response to such comments was a violation of her First Amendment rights.

For the following reasons, we affirm the Plaintiff's claim and order further proceedings.[2216]

This case is about Dick Taylor and Robert Taylor, as Plaintiff's, filing suit against Chief of Police Phillip Keith, of Knoxville, Tennessee, in August of 2008.

The Plaintiffs, police officers Dick Taylor and Robert Taylor, brought a civil rights action against the Defendant, which included the Chief of Police as well as several Knoxville supervisory police officers. The Taylor's allege that the Defendant's retaliated against them for the exercise for their First Amendment rights.

On December 14, 1997, the Plaintiff, Robert Taylor, was serving a Warrant on Jack Longmire. He resisted arrest and in the course of the struggle, the Plaintiff called for emergency assistance and was accidentally sprayed with pepper spray. The officers' eventually placed Longmire in handcuffs, forced him onto the ground, and then put him into the squad car. Officer Taylor's father, Dick Taylor, responded to the emergency call. Other officers' arrived on the scene and were told that Longmire resisted arrest, which was followed by a struggle. Longmire was treated for some wounds by the arriving officers. The second Plaintiff, Dick Taylor, ordered another officer to clean up some blood on the pavement. When Mrs. Longmire expressed some concern regarding her husband's beating, Plaintiff Taylor told her she could file an Abuse Complaint with Internal Affairs.

An internal investigation of the incident took place, with the Chief of Police as well as the Deputy Chief conducting the inquiry. At the conclusion of the investigation, the Plaintiffs were both terminated, with charges of covering up the incident.

The city alleged that the Plaintiff failed to take proper action regarding allegations of Officer abuse and improperly processed evidence when he washed away Longmire's blood without calling Criminal Logistics to process the scene.

The Plaintiffs' filed a grievance regarding their terminations. After a hearing, the Administrative Hearing Officer, found overwhelming evidence that the investigation was initiated as a result of the Use of Force Report prepared by the Plaintiff, and renewed upon concerns expressed by the Plaintiff at a later date. This evidence, the Hearing Officer concluded, was wholly inconsistent with the City's allegations that the Plaintiffs' attempted to cover up the Longmire beating incident. The Plaintiffs' were ordered to be reinstated, with back pay.

The Defendant's appealed the decision of the Hearing Officer to the Tennessee Court of Appeals, which overturned the original decision, in part. The Plaintiffs' were reinstated, but incurred thirty-day suspensions.

The Plaintiff's filed their Federal Suit, citing retaliation against them for exercising their First Amendment rights. Specifically, the Taylor's claim they were wrongfully fired for refusing to remain silent, and upon reinstatement, were subjected to further retaliation (loss of clothing and equipment; increased scheduling of holidays and weekends, and denial of training and career advancement opportunities, which continues to this day.

The Court has ruled that public employees have a Constitutional right to comment on matters of public concern. Public employers cannot silence their employees simply because they disapprove of their speech. Although it was not necessary for the Plaintiffs' to have spoken to the press, or to the general public in order for their speech to be protected, some part of their speech must touch upon public concern. Speech touches upon a matter of public concern if it can be fairly considered to be relating to any matter of political, social, or other concern to the community. However, when a public employee speaks, not as a citizen upon matters of public concern, but instead as an employee upon matters of personal interest, his speech is not afforded any Constitutional protections.

Whether an employee's speech addresses a matter of public concern, must be determined by the content, form, and content of a given statement, as revealed by the record as a whole. The essence of the Plaintiff's argument is that the content of their speech alleged police brutality, addresses a matter of public concern. Moreover, they assert that their speech should be afforded Constitutional protection because its purpose was "to bring to light actual or potential wrongdoing, or breach of public trust."

In essence, the Plaintiff's speech was intended to communicate the potential wrongdoing of a fellow officer. The Plaintiff's report implicating a fellow officer's use of excessive force reaches the level of public concern. The Plaintiff's report contained facts, not accusations. The purpose of this report was to bring to light conduct that warranted further investigation to ensure that the arrest was being carried out according to the law. In Marohnic v. Walker, <u>Holding that statements regarding the operation of public organizations in accordance with the law, are matters of public concern.</u>

The Plaintiffs' have presented adequate evidence suggesting that the Defendant's actions were partially motivated by their desire to silence them about the excessive force incident. The Taylor's, who observed the excessive force incident, were the only officers' who filed a complaint. Other officers', who were present and witnessed the incident, did not follow-up with written reports and were not disciplined by their Supervisors' for failure to report excessive officer force.

In reviewing the evidence, it is reasonable for the Court to conclude that the disparate treatment of the officers involved in the excessive force incident, shows that the Department targeted the Plaintiffs' because of their speech.

Therefore, the Court remands the case for further proceedings.[2227]

This profile case involves Keith Dambrot v. Central Michigan University. The suit was filed in 1995.

On May 12, 1991, Dambrot became Head Basketball Coach of the Central Michigan University's men's team. The lawsuit arises from events which occurred during the 1992-93 basketball season. The 1992 team was made up of eleven African-Americans and three Caucasians.

In January of 1993, the Plaintiff used the "N"-word during a locker-room session with his players' during a half-time break, during a game where his team did not play very well. The Plaintiff Coach told the players' that they were not playing very well. He asked them, "Do you mind if I use the "N" word?" After some of the players' said it was okay, the Plaintiff said, "You know we need to have more "N" players' on our team." The Coach pointed out one of the white players', "Plays like a "N". He's hard-nosed and tough". The Coach later testified he intended to use the term in a positive and reinforcing manner. The player's often referred to each other with the "N" word. The Plaintiff stated he used the "N" word in the same manner in which the players' used the term amongst themselves, "to connote a person who is fearless, mentally strong, and tough."

The news that the Plaintiff Coach had used the "N" word in the locker-room incident became common knowledge to others' at the University. In February of 1993, the team was interviewed by the press at the request of the Plaintiff. The African-American players, who were interviewed, said they were not offended by the Coach's use of the term. However, a former player of the team did complain to the University's Affirmative Action Officer. The Affirmative Action Officer (AAO) confronted the Plaintiff, who admitted using the word, but stated he used it in a positive manner. However, the AAO viewed the Plaintiff's use of the "N"- word as a violation of the University's Discriminatory Harassment Policy, and recommended that Dambrot be disciplined. The Plaintiff accepted the proposed disciplinary action, in lieu of a more formal investigation. The Plaintiff was suspended without pay for five days.

News of the locker-room incident and the Plaintiff's suspension, spread throughout the campus. The Plaintiff's further public statements were characterized as more explanatory and defensive, rather than apologetic in tone. Students staged demonstrations with considerable regional and national media coverage of the incident at CMU.

On April 12, 1993, the Athletic Director informed the Plaintiff Coach, that he would not be retained as Head Coach for the 1993-94 season.

The Plaintiff filed a lawsuit on April 19, 1993, alleging he was fired because he used the "N"-word, and the termination violated is First Amendment right of free speech and academic freedom. Several members of the team joined the lawsuit, alleging the University's Discriminatory Harassment Policy was overboard and vague and violated First Amendment rights. The University's Discriminatory Harassment Policy is unconstitutional on its face.

The parties are allowed to bring an action under the First Amendment, based on a belief that a certain statute or policy is so broad as to "chill" the exercise of free speech and expression. A policy or statute is unconstitutional on its face, or overboard on grounds, if there is "a realistic danger that the statute itself will significantly compromise recognized First Amendment protections of parties not before the Court.

The language of CMU's policy is sweeping and seemingly drafted to include as much and as many types of conduct as possible. On its face, the policy reaches a "substantial amount of constitutionally protected speech." The broad scope of the policy's language presents a real danger that the University could compromise the protection afforded by the First Amendment.

What the University cannot do, however, was establish an anti-discrimination policy which had the effect of prohibiting certain speech because it disagreed with ideas or messages thought to be offensive, even gravely so, by large numbers of people.

The overboard policy of Discriminatory Harassment may impose on constitutionally protected speech such as in Marohnic, "Statements regarding operations of public organizations such as Universities in accordance with the law, are a matter of public concern."

For the foregoing reasons, in favor of the Plaintiffs' finding the CMU Discriminatory Harassment Policy violates the First Amendment. We order further Court proceedings.[2238]

In the next case, David Charvat began working as the Superintendent of EORWA, a Waste Water Treatment Plant on the Ohio River that serves four municipalities. The Plaintiff began his employment on July 5, 1994. The Plaintiff assumed his position unaware of the water treatment facility's non-compliance with various environmental regulations.

In addition, the Plaintiff soon uncovered additional problems at the facility. A facility pump discharge unit was "Jimmy-rigged", which resulted in the potential of raw sewage to be discharged into the public water supply. The Plaintiff also became aware that earlier, the facility management had evaded enforcement by failing to report its regulatory violations to the DEPA.

In July of 1994, the Plaintiff attended his first Board Meeting. He reported to them that the Plant had operational problems that required immediate attention; that staff morale was low, and that he intended to improve communications with the Federal Regulators. He also requested support from the Board to conduct an engineering study of the Plant. During the next few months, the Board took no action on his repeated requests. Additionally, employees of the Plant were not accustomed to reporting violations under the previous Superintendent. The Plaintiff claims that the employees feared they would lose their jobs if they reported Plant violations.

The Plaintiff's actions resulted in greater reporting of permit violations. The DEPA notified the Plaintiff that they were reopening a 1993 investigation of the Plant. Shortly thereafter, a Plant Board Member called the Plaintiff to express his anger that the Plaintiff's actions had caused the new investigation by the EPA. The Board Member also allegedly stated he would not have his political career ruined by the sewage authority. The Plaintiff continued to believe that the Plant was still operating in violation of the law and that many Plant staff were discouraged from reporting violations

The rancor between the Plaintiff and the Board intensified from January, 1995 to his termination in September, 1995. In May of 1995, the Board informed the Plaintiff that he had ninety days to improve staff employee morale and Plant operations.

In June of 1995, The Ohio Attorney General's Office notified the Plant that they would conduct an investigation of the facility, with possible civil fines. Aware of the gravity of the situation, the Plaintiff sent a letter to the Board, strongly suggesting they disclose all known violations of the Plant. He also urged the Board to order an internal investigation to uncover the extent of the violations.

The Plaintiff maintains that his letter to the Board constituted protected speech under the First Amendment yet was a substantial cause of the Board's decision to terminate him later that year. The Board held a special meeting to discuss the Plaintiff's letter, and the Board decided to exclude the Plaintiff from meeting with the Ohio Attorney General, and from participating in the Plant's negotiations with the Ohio authorities.

The Plaintiff alleges that the Board devised a plan to submit to the Ohio Attorney General, that the Board was unaware of the extent of the violations. The Board also instructed all Plant employees not to talk to the Ohio Attorney General's investigators. Employees would need approval from the Board before speaking to the Ohio Attorney General. The Board also admitted that the Plaintiff would be fired if he spoke to the Ohio Attorney General about Plant violations.

Meanwhile, the Plaintiff's efforts to discover, report, and correct Plant violations created tension among the employees. As a result, the Board invited all employees' to a meeting to express their complaints about the Plaintiff. Only one employee attended the meeting, and did not complain too strongly about the Plaintiff.

In August of 1995, The Board voted to begin termination proceedings against the Plaintiff. Fifteen grounds were listed to justify termination. The reasons mostly involved complaints about the Plaintiff's management skills and his failure to follow orders from the Board. The Board held an Executive Session and voted to fire him. The Plaintiff filed a complaint with the Department of Labor, claiming he was fired due to his reporting of Plant violations to the Board and the EPA.

The Administrative Law Judge rules that the Plaintiff's termination was a pretext to mask the Board's unlawful motives of preventing the Plaintiff from reporting regulatory violations. As a result of these findings, the Attorney General ordered the Board to reinstate the Plaintiff as Superintendent with $175,000.00 back pay and $5,000.00 for emotional stress.

The Plaintiff filed suit in Federal Court in September of 1997, against the Board, claiming violations of his First Amendment rights. He claims his termination was in retaliation for his exercise of his free speech rights.

The Defendant's argued that the Plaintiff's speech, as cited by his letter to the Board pinpointing Plant violations, was speech relating to personnel issues and internal operations, was inaccurate at best. The Plaintiff reports about the sewage treatment facility's violations of a number of environmental regulations. When analyzed for their content, form and context, the reports are a perfect example of protected speech that is designed to increase the awareness of regulatory violations and potential threats to the public health and safety of the community. This Court has declared that the "public interest is near its zenith when ensuring that public organizations are being operated in accordance with the law", Marohnic v Walker.

The Defendants also argue that the Plaintiff decreased employee morale by openly criticizing the Plant operations. They claim his speech did not outweigh the interests of the State which promotes efficiency. The Board members' maintained that they were required to restrain the Plaintiff's speech in order to safeguard the efficiency of the Plant's day to day operations. They again miss the point with this contention. The Plaintiff's duties as Superintendent of the Water Treatment Facility, included more than managing its employees; of at least equal importance was ensuring that the Plant complied with environmental regulations.

Having concluded that the Plaintiff's speech did reach matters of public concern, it seems clear that the Plaintiff has met this burden for establishing a case for retaliation.[2249]

This situation demonstrates workplace related speech that DOES NOT reach the level of protected speech afforded by the First Amendment. Even though the Plaintiff did not prevail, it does not detract from the degree of courage and passion displayed by the Plaintiff in pursuing redress. However, the Courts' must insure decisions remain within the zone of reaching levels of "public concern".

Denise Welsbarth began her employment with the Ohio State Park System as a Park Ranger in 2003. The Plaintiff led an initiative to institute a canine-handling team and eventually became the Department's official Canine Handler. The Plaintiff alleges that the Department as a whole, began suffering "serious morale and performance" problems in 2003. Management responded to these problems by having a paid Consultant to evaluate the Department. As part of the evaluation, the Consultant rode along with the Plaintiff in her patrol vehicle during her shift. The Plaintiff's First Amendment complaint is based solely on the conversation that took place during the ride-along.

The first topic the Plaintiff discussed was a disciplinary letter of reprimand that the Plaintiff had recently received. The Plaintiff told the Consultant she was going to write a letter of rebuttal, to be placed within her Personnel File. The second topic discussed by the Plaintiff, were the morale and performance problems within the Department. Later, the Consultant reported these comments made by the Plaintiff to the Park District as an expression of a personal dislike for her co-workers.

The Plaintiff contends that because of her ride-along conversations, the Consultant labeled her "a source of friction".

During this time, the Plaintiff had an unexcused absence from work and was cited for that absence. The Management Staff also ordered that she have psychological testing, based on her alleged irrational behavior on the job. The results of the testing deemed her unfit for duty. The Plaintiff sought a second evaluation through her Union, which found her to be fit for duty. In response, the Park Officials' ordered a third, tie-breaking test, which concurred with the first test, deeming her unfit for duty.

The Plaintiff filed a grievance with the Union, and the Arbitrator agreed with her. The Hearing Officer asked that both parties try to work out a settlement.

The Plaintiff filed a First Amendment suit in 2005. In order for a public employee's speech to be protected, the Supreme Court have long imposed two threshold requirements, (1) Plaintiff must have spoken as a citizen, and (2) Addressed a matter of public concern.

To begin with, the Plaintiff did not speak as a citizen. The ride-along conversations with the Consultant centered on morale and performance issues. This would not fall under the domain of protected speech.

The Plaintiff's reliance on Marohnic v. Walker, in which this Court reversed a grant of Summary Judgment in favor of the employer, regarding a First Amendment retaliation claim is misplaced. The Court in that case, found the employee's speech to be protected where he spoke to police officers' regarding a criminal investigation of his employer, a State Mental Health Board. In fact, the Court emphasized that Marohnic's speech was induced by civic commitment "to cooperate with law enforcement", rather than by any official duty related to his employment. Marohnic thus differs materially from the present scenario where the Plaintiff spoke solely about Departmental morale and performance issues to a Consultant hired by the Park Officials.

The Plaintiff's speech only addressed issues of workplace disputes and poor employee morale, and therefore did not reach the threshold of protected speech, because it did not touch upon matters of public concern. Because of these factors, the Plaintiff cannot prevail.[3250]

In the next scenario, Christine Brandenberg, former Executive Director of the Housing Authority of Irvine, Kentucky, brought suit claiming her former employer violated her First Amendment rights by retaliating against her for engaging in protected speech.

The Housing Authority, created by Kentucky law, is responsible for the planning and management of public housing in Irvine, Kentucky. The United States Department of Housing and Urban Development regulates the Housing Authority.

The Plaintiff's position as Executive Director required her to work closely with the Board. In-fighting and dysfunction were therefore the inevitable consequences, when tensions began to manifest in 1992 between the Plaintiff and the Board. The Board claims that the Plaintiff became hostile, and sometimes would shout at Board Members. The Board alleges the Plaintiff bought a van without authorization from the Board. The relationship between the Board and the Plaintiff became very contentious.

The degree of hostility between the Board and the Plaintiff intensified to the point that the Plaintiff took a leave of absence and shortly thereafter, resigned.

The Court ruled that the Plaintiff's speech did touch upon matters of public concern, satisfying the first part of the complaint, but the Court determined the Housing Authority's interest in efficient administration of its public housing projects, outweighed the Plaintiff's interest in publicly commenting on Board Members' possible misconduct.

Accordingly, the District Court held that the Plaintiff failed to prove an essential element of her First Amendment retaliation claim, and the Housing Authority was entitled to Judgment, as a matter of law. We also present a question on whether the Plaintiff's speech touched upon a matter of public concern. In general, speech involves a matter of public concern when it involves issues about which information is needed to enable the members of society to make informed decisions about the operation of their government.

Such matters of public concern are to be contrasted with internal personnel disputes or complaints about an employers' performance.

Generally, the public interest is near its zenith when ensuring that public organizations are being operated in accordance with the law. Marohnic v. Walker. Here the Plaintiff's speech concerned three subjects, (1) Her criticism of the Board's decision to demolish a public housing unit, (2) Her belief that moving administrative offices to another location would be a misuse pf money, and (3) Her concern about Board Members having conflicts of interest.

Her speech, like many personal employee grievances, appeared to be motivated by self-interest, rather than public concern.

Therefore, we rule in favor of the Housing Authority.[3261]

Sharon Gragg, in 1996, was employed by the Kentucky Department of Technical Education (DTE). She was a Regional Educational Consultant at the Somerset Technical College. Gragg's Supervisor was Anne Cline, the Director of the Southern Region of the DTE.

Due to budget cuts, the DTE began planning for the elimination of several positions within the Department. One of the positions selected for elimination was Plaintiff Gragg's, according to the Department.

The Plaintiff participated in informal pre-termination hearings, after which her Attorney sent a letter to the DTE General Counsel, contesting the decision to eliminate Gragg's position.

The Plaintiff was laid off in October of 1996. She filed an appeal, charging gender and age discrimination with the Equal Employment Opportunity Commission (EOC). The Plaintiff's complaint against the Cabinet alleges that she had been terminated in retaliation for her exercising her rights under the Kentucky Constitution and the First Amendment. She further claimed her termination was in violation of State and Federal law, prohibiting discrimination in employment on the basis of gender and age, and in violation of the Kentucky Whistleblower Act.

Germane to this case are the Plaintiff's claims that the Defendants' eliminated her position because, during the course of her employment, she had pointed out areas of deficiency and of concern, and had been critical of the Defendant's administrative decisions.

Gragg claims the Defendants' terminated her employment because she exercised her First Amendment right of free speech. In order for the Plaintiff to prevail, she must demonstrate that she was engaged in a Constitutionally protected activity, and that the Defendants' adverse action caused her to suffer an injury that would likely chill a person of ordinary firmness from continuing to engage in that activity, and that the adverse action was motivated, at least in part, as a response to the exercise of her Constitutional rights.

The Plaintiff fails at the first step. Speech is protected when it addresses a matter of public concern and the employee's interest in making such statements outweighs the "interest of the State, as an employer, in promoting the efficiency of the public service it performs through its employees."

The Plaintiff argues that her speech was a matter of public concern, relying heavily on the assertion that she was criticizing the allegedly improper functioning of her Agency employer, and the improper allocation of public monies. However, the fact that an issue involves public money is alone not enough to convert express activity into commentary on a matter of public concern. Nor does a matter become one of public concern simply because; in other circumstances its subject matter might be of public interest. The point of the protection afforded public employees' is to allow public employees' a voice on issues actually affecting, and interesting to the community at large.

General administrative errors made during a staff study of the Department, and cited by the Plaintiff, were less grand issues, such as errors in data reporting that did not even reach a level of public exposure. Unlike other circumstances where the Court has determined that Employee's speech referred to a matter of public concern--exercising a public Agency's fraud, see Marohnic v. Walker.

However, in this case, the matters brought to the public eye were internal grievances unrelated to larger issues of public policy. Many of the administrative and personnel violations cited by the Plaintiff, may be involving misappropriation of public funds, was not attempting to expose fraud and corruption--or even relatively wrong doing or error--on the part of the Agency; rather the Plaintiff was simply advising the employees' who believe they were being denied proper grievance procedures.

In short, we conclude that all of the speech the Plaintiff points as protected, falls outside the public realm. The Plaintiff's complaints are well within the characterization of the Connick ruling of the Supreme Court that stated: "To presume that all matters which transpire within a government office are of public concern would mean that virtually every mark--and certainly every criticism directed at a public official, would plant the seed of a Constitutional case. While as a matter of good judgment, public officials' should be receptive to constructive criticism offered by their employees', the First Amendment does not require a public office to run as a roundtable for employee complaints over internal office affairs."

We therefore, hold that in light of the Plaintiff's failure to demonstrate that any Constitutional right was violated at all, the Plaintiff claims that her employment was terminated in retaliation for her exercising her right to free speech, must be dismissed.[3272]

LAW JOURNAL REVIEW

In concluding this Chapter, we will attempt to illustrate the "rippling waves" effect captured through a sampling of Law Journals discussing the key requirements of what constitutes "matters of public concern" as a prerequisite for meeting the Constitutional standard of protected speech.

To begin, the First Amendment is a Constitutional principle that needs the Court System to reach its fruition. We look to case litigations and Court rulings to discern what is, and what is not, matters of public concern, before validating what is protected speech.[3284]

The Case Law Books and Law Journals, highlight an extensive series of hallmark cases, including the Marohnic v. Walker, Sixth Circuit Court ruling, which all have advanced the clarion call for free speech liberties by constant shaping and defining what is constitutionally protected speech.

In this context, the first question to ask is, how does the First Amendment protect public employees? The First Amendment to the U. S. Constitution states, The Congress shall have no laws respecting an establishment of religion or prohibiting the free exercise thereof, or abridging the freedom of speech or of the press or the right of the people peaceably to assemble, and to petition the government for redress of grievances.[3295]

One thing to know about the First Amendment is that there is a limit only on government. It restricts the State from passing laws that infringe on the rights of religion, speech, press, assembly, and petition.[3306]

However, if your employer is a private entity, you have no protections from being fired, based on your speech. You may be protected by other sources, such as binding arbitration, Unions, and State and Local Civil Service laws. In general, the Courts have ruled that First Amendment protections can apply if; (1) The Plaintiff was engaged in protected activity, (2) That the Defendants' adverse action caused the Plaintiff to suffer an injury that would likely chill a persons' ordinary firmness from continuing to engage in that activity, and (3) That the adverse action motivated at least in part, as a response to the exercise of the Plaintiff's Constitutional rights.[3317]

For a public employee to claim retaliation by the Supervisor, the Court must also find: (4) That the employee's speech was a matter of public concern, (5) The interest of the employee as a citizen in commenting on matters of public concern, outweighs the employer's interest in promoting efficiency of the public service it performs through its employees.[3328]

What is speech that defines public concern? Public elections, pending legislation, corruption, misuse of public funds, discrimination, and public health and safety, are top priorities.[3339]

Areas that do not fall within the zones of protected speech are internal personal grievances, office politics, and employer-employee conflicts focusing on promotion denials, etc. Also comments of self-interest regarding work related disputes, fall short of protected speech.[4340]

In addition, definitions too broad as to what constitutes "public concern" may frustrate employer legitimate disciplinary measures by litigating frivolous free speech complaints.[4351]

To avoid this problem, the Courts have designed a legal test that burdens the employee by requiring him to demonstrate that the speech fits neatly in a well-defined area of public concern. For example, the Marohnic case involving a public employee cooperating with a State Medicaid fraud investigation, meets the proper definition of public concern.[4362]

In closing, established case law precedents, as well as corresponding Law Journal reviews, have broken down the Constitutional principle of free speech liberties into applied and workable law constructs that allow for Court adjudications which are designed to fulfill the ultimate promise of the First Amendment. The ebb and flow of First Amendment Court litigations separate the wheat from the chaff, so as to define what constitutes constitutionally protected speech.

When faced with a workplace situation of irresolvable wrongdoing, the three courses of action which one faces are, (1) Put your job security first and foremost; keep your mouth shut, and go along with things as they are; (2) Get out of the situation. Locate another employment opportunity, leaving the old workplace while you are in good standing, but knowing in your heart of hearts that the corruption will continue or even escalate, or (3) Take a stand for what is right. Collect your evidence and take the plunge to report the improper practices. Commit to see things through to a just end.

The act of reporting wrongdoing in itself may not insure that it will be deemed as protected speech by the Courts, no matter what the degree of risk is involved. Those who elect to take what they believe is the morally correct pathway, thus placing themselves in jeopardy, do not enthusiastically or fervently do so. In fact, putting oneself at odds with their employer often is viewed by some to be reckless, or even foolish.

However, on occasion, the workplace circumstances compel them to take what may be considered to be an unpopular or controversial stance, most often resulting in certain reprisals and retribution.

Our revealing stories depict this clash between employee values and employer expediency, with no guarantees of legal protection. In the final analysis, our profiles in courage case studies, give a picture of those who committed to a cause, and to the promise of the First Amendment.

As we have noted, protected speech validated only by the Federal Courts, must overcome a difficult threshold to obtain the coveted mantel of U. S. Constitution protection. As a whistleblower, to me and to the many others who have shared their stories, receiving the mantle of protected speech has had an enduring special meaning.

Chapter VII

Epilogue

At long last the protracted ordeal had come to an end! Our whistleblowing with very reputed voicings will be slow to fade from community memory. However, within the wider public domain our story will endure for perpetuity.

Yet for all practical purposes, life must go on. For better or worse, a stigma will often precede all whistleblowers in their future job pursuit efforts. Fortunately, Dick and Madelyn eventually were able to restart their stalled careers, and enjoy much success within their respective chosen professions. As for me, my career in Social Work administration proved to be short lived. Too many bridges were burned as a result of continued employer reprisals which ultimately put a halt to new employment possibilities.

My once promising career now in shambles; at forty years old, I found myself unemployable in my chosen field. My outlook about my future was bleak. It didn't take long for me to realize my circumstances were so bad, only Divine intervention could turn things around. So I prayed fervently for a deeper faith in God's plan for me; placing my fate in His hands. Oddly, before long I sensed a soul penetrating calmness and an emotional assurance, that better days were to come.

Soon the winds of change became evident, when I secured the winning bid on a choice historic rural farm property in Southern

Kentucky. The acquisition of this small farm abundantly changed life as I knew it. The sudden shift from city dwelling to the quieter lifestyle of the country would be the catalyst for transformation. I needed more than a mere reboot; my life required a rebirth. I shed the shackles of persistent insecurity, uncertainty, and long restless nights; as without hesitation I embraced the prospect of a new life fashioned by God.

This seventeen acre farm, rich in history dating back to the early 18th century, was like a beacon offering the promising and rewarding future I so desperately desired. This became the zenith of my rebirth.

During the following three decades, and well into the 21st century, I would have the opportunity to truly live a renaissance life. I had the occasion to wear many hats as the time passed. I was a farmer, a Bed and Breakfast Innkeeper, owner and steward of a landmark Native American Sacred Site Cave, horse rescuer, and a writer of sorts.

I have a life I could never have imagined; full and extraordinarily blessed.

Endnotes

1. Mental Health System Act, Public Law 96-398, October 7, 1980

2. Marohnic v. Walker, United States Court of Appeals, Sixth Circuit, September 10, 1986

3. Mental Health Systems Act, Public Law 96-398, pg.1593: Sec. 407 paragraph (5)

4. U.S. House, Congressional Record, 7603, Rep. Tim Lee Carter Speech, August 22, 1980

5. Mental Health Systems Act, Public Law 96-398, Sec. 407 (3), October 7,1980

6. Park City Daily News, "Job Action Results In New Law", Bowling Green, KY., October 16, 1980

7. Marohnic v. Walker, U. S. Court of Appeals, Sixth Circuit, September 10, 1986

8. Marohnic v. Walker, U. S. Court of Appeals, Sixth Circuit, September 10, 1986

9. CPA Journal, "Whistle blowing and Good Governance," Tim V. Eaton and Michael Akers, June 2007

10. CPA Journal, "Whistle blowing and Good Governance", Tim V. Eaton and Michael Akers, June 2007

11. Garcetti v. Ceballos, Brief for Respondent, U. S. Supreme Court, July 2005

12. Rep. Tim Lee Carter statement, Committee of Interstate and Foreign Commerce, August 22, 1980

13. Tate and Runner, "First Amendment Rights of Public Employees, www.workplacefairness/index, retailationpublic. *Marohnic v Walker, 800 F 2d, 613-616, 6th Cir., 1986.*

14. Wilkin v. Jakeway, 94-4137 "(Sixth Circuit), 1996. *Marohnic v. Walker, 800 F 2d, 613-616, 6th Cir., 1986.*

15. Terry J. Wilkins v. Donald E. Jakeway, U. S. Court of Appeals, Sixth Circuit, 1996, No. 94-4137. *Marohnic v. Walker, 800 F 2d, 613-616, 6th Cir., 1986.*

16. Clyde Conway v. Edward C. Smith, City of Kansas City, Kansas, U. S. Court of Appeals, Tenth Circuit, 1988, No. 85-2914. *Marohnic v. Walker, 800 F 2d, 613-616, 6th Cir., 1986.*

17. Everett Perry v. Kenneth McGinnis, U. S. Court of Appeals, Sixth Circuit, 2000, No. 98-1607. *Marohnic v. Walker, 800 F 2d, 613-616, 6th Cir., 1986.*

18. Carolyn T. Rogers v. Elizabeth Banks, U. S. Court of Appeals, Sixth Circuit, 2003, No. 01-4034. *Marohnic v. Walker, 800 F 2d, 613-616, 6th Cir., 1986.*

19. Deborah Kaye Hudson v. Washington County, Tennessee, Susan Mitchell Stanley, U.S. Court of Appeals, Sixth Circuit, 1993, No. 92-5763. *Marohnic v. Walker, 800 F 2d, 613-616, 6th Cir., 1986.*

20. Hetzel D. See v. City of Elyria, Chief Michael Medders, U. S. Court of Appeals, Sixth Circuit, 2007, No. 06-4195. *Marohnic v. Walker, 800 F 2d, 613-616, 6th Cir., 1986.*

21. Paul Hatfield, Fred McCoy v. Charles "Fuzzy" Keesee, U. S. Court of Appeals, Sixth Circuit, 1993, No. 92-5636. *Marohnic v. Walker, 800 F 2d, 613-616, 6th Cir., 1986.*

22. Odis Solomon v. Royal Oak Township, Tommy Stannton, U. S. Court of Appeals, Sixth Circuit, 1988. *Marohnic v. Walker, 800 F 2d, 613-616, 6th Cir., 1986.*

23. Dale D. Hoover v. Patricia Radabulsh, U. S. Court of Appeals, Sixth Circuit, 2002, No. 00-4537. *Marohnic v. Walker, 800 F 2d, 613-616, 6th Cir., 1986.*

24. Julia Ward v. Eastern Michigan University, U. S. Court of Appeals, Sixth Circuit, 2010. *Marohnic v. Walker, 800 F 2d, 613-616, 6th Cir., 1986.*

25. Carolyn Modica v. Clare Taylor, Antoinette Humphrey, U. S. Court of Appeals, Fifth Circuit, 2006, No. 05-50075. *Marohnic v. Walker, 800 F 2d, 613-616, 6th Cir., 1986.*

26. Julie Pucci v. Nineteenth District Court, City of Dearborn, Judge Mark W. Somners, U. S. Court of Appeals, Sixth Circuit, 2009, No. 08-2017. *Marohnic v. Walker, 800 F 2d, 613-616, 6th Cir., 1986.*

27. Taylor and Taylor v. Chief of Police Phillip Keith, U. S. Court of Appeals, Sixth Circuit, 2003, No. 01-6460. *Marohnic v. Walker, 800 F 2d, 613-616, 6th Cir., 1986.*

28. Keith Dambrot, Laketh Boyd v. Central Michigan University, U. S. Court of Appeals, Sixth Circuit, 1995, No. 94-1015. *Marohnic v. Walker, 800 F 2d, 613-616, 6th Cir., 1986.*

29. David Charvat v. Eastern Ohio Regional Water Authority, U. S. Court of Appeals, Sixth Circuit, 2001, No. 00-3431; *Marohnic v. Walker, 800 F2d, 613-616, 6th Cir., 1986.*

30. Denise Welsbarth v. Geauga Park District, U. S. District Court, Northern District of Ohio, No. 02928,2007. *Marohnic v. Walker, 800 F 2d, 613-616, 6th Cir., 1986.*

31. Christine Brandenburg v. Housing Authority of Irvine, U. S. District Court, Eastern District of Kentucky, 2001, U. S. Court of Appeals, Sixth Circuit, No. 99-6-6308-396. *Marohnic v. Walker, 800 F 2d, 613-616, 6th Cir., 1986.*

32. Sharon L. Gragg v. Kentucky Cabinet for Workforce Development: Somerset Technical College, U.S. Court of Appeals, Sixth Circuit, 2002, No. 01-5171. *Marohnic v. Walker, 800 F2d, 613-616, 6th Cir., 1986.*

33. First Amendment Rights of Public employees, Tate and Renner, 2010. *Marohnic v. Walker, 800 F2d, 613-616, 6th Cir, 1986.*

34. The First Amendment and Public Sector Labor Relations, William Herbert, *The Labor Lawyer,* Vol. 19, Number 3 Winter/2004. *Marohnic v. Walker, 800 F2d, 613-616, 6th Cir., 1986 .* American Bar Association.

35. First Amendment Rights of Public Employees, Tate and Renner, 2010. *Marohnic v. Walker, 800 F 2d, 613-616, 6th Cir., 1986.*

36. Article: Permissible Content Discrimination under the First Amendment: The Strange Case of the Public Employee, Lawrence Rosenthal, Hastings College of Law, *Hastings Constitutional Law Quarterly,* Summer/1998. *Marohnic v. Walker, 800 F2d, 613-616, 6th Cir.,1986.*

37. Protections For Public Employees who "Blow The Whistle" Appear To Be Inadequate, William Herbert, New York State Bar Association, Feb. 2004. Vol.76, No. 2. *Marohnic v. Walker, 800 F2d, 613-616, 6th Cir., 1986.*

38. First Amendment Rights of Public Employees, Tate and Renner, 2010. *Marohnic v. Walker, 800 F2d, 613-616, 6th Cir., 1986.*

39. Article: Permissible Content Discrimination Under The First Amendment: The Strange Case of the Public Employee, Lawrence Rosenthal, Hastings College of Law *Hastings Constitutional Law Quarterly,* Summer/1998. *Marohnic v. Walker, 800 F2d, 613-616, 6*[th] *Cir., 1986.*

40. Connick to Confusion: The Struggle to Define Speech on Matters of Public Concern, Stephen Allred, *Indiana Law Journal,* 1998. *Marohnic v. Walker, 800 F2d, 613-616, 6*[th] *Cir., 1986.*

41. Connick to Confusion: The Struggle to Define Speech on Matters of Public Concern, Stephen Allred, *Indiana Law Journal,* 1998. *Marohnic v. Walker, 800 F2d, 613-616, 6*[th] *Cir., 1986.*

Acknowledgements

On a personal note, I wish to begin by thanking Madelyn McGuire and Richard Hayes for their unwavering support throughout the entire difficult years. Their steadfast assistance during the reporting of wrongdoing, cooperation with the State investigation, and as co-litigant plaintiffs, was essential to the positive outcome realized.

In addition, I would like to acknowledge the late Congressman Tim Lee Carter (R 1965-1981) of Tompkinsville, Kentucky for his critical advocacy which led to Federal Legislation reform, known as "The Whistleblower Protection Clause", which was inspired by our case and which he addressed so eloquently, on the floor of the U. S. House of Representatives, August 22, 1980. This protection clause was included in the massive MENTAL HEALTH SYSTEMS ACT or PUBLIC LAW 96-398, passed by the United States Congress and subsequently signed into law on October 7, 1980, by President Jimmy Carter.

Additionally, special recognition is given to Attorney Tom Noe III, of Russellville, Kentucky, who represented me in successfully arguing the merits of my case before the United States Sixth Circuit Court of Appeals in1986. This Federal case, known as Marohnic v. Walker, resulted in First Amendment Case Law further protecting free speech litigation for all those reporting wrong doing by government agencies.

Special thanks to Professor Chuck Hormann, of the School of Social Work, University of Kentucky. Even after thirty-five years, I still recall as an educator, how inspiring he was to all of his students. He always impressed upon us the need to accept any unknown future challenges we would face, with commitment and compassion. To apply the mind as well as the heart to the fullest, as Social Workers, was his constant theme. These enduring principles remained a steadfast beacon for me during dark and challenging times.

My gratitude is extended to Mr. William Bohnert, the Warden of the Blackburn Correctional Prison, near Lexington, Kentucky. As my first boss, he set me on the right path in my Social Work journey.

Moreover, I want to acknowledge my sincere appreciation to a good friend and great farmer, the late Mr. Haz Ballance, of Oakland, Kentucky. Haz inspired me to get more in touch with the land and nature. Over the years, this has brought me much peace and tranquility.

Not least of all, I acknowledge my lifelong friend Robert J. Craig, who followed his own star; thus setting an example for us all. Bob passed from this life in 2019. He knew of my gratitude to him for standing by me as I struggled through the tedious court battles. I miss him every day.

I especially thank God for His guidance in leading me daily.

Additional Recommended Readings

....**The Secret Grotto/Dare to Believe!** William J. Marohnic, Amazon.com 2018

....**Eye on the Sparrow** William J. Marohnic, Amazon.com 2014

....**How I Became a Horse Rescuer** William J. Marohnic, Amazon.com 2016

....**The Miracle of the Conscience/A Portal to The Heavens** William J Marohnic, Amazon.com 2010

Author's Bio

Bill Marohnic has been a resident of Kentucky for 50 years. He is a graduate of the University Of Kentucky School Of Social Work. Bill enjoys time spent on his small South Central Kentucky farm where he serves as Innkeeper for the family's Bed and Breakfast business. He is a long time horse rescuer of local renown, and a proud Grandfather to Dylan and Hannah.

www.ingramcontent.com/pod-product-compliance
Lightning Source LLC
Chambersburg PA
CBHW050530280326
41933CB00011B/1533